# The Indomital
## The 1946 Rugby League Li
## Australia and New Ze

Gus Risman leads out the team at Junee in the first tour match. (DP)

# Colin Thomson

# London League Publications Ltd

## The Indomitables
## The 1946 Rugby League Lions tour of
## Australia and New Zealand

First published in Great Britain in April 2009 by:
London League Publications Ltd, P.O. Box 10441, London E14 8WR

ISBN:                    978-1903659-44-1

Cover design by:         Stephen McCarthy Graphic Design
                         46, Clarence Road, London N15 5BB

Layout:                  Peter Lush

Printed in Great Britain: by the MPG Books Group
                         Bodmin and King's Lynn

# Foreword

Being invited to write the foreword to this historic and eagerly awaited book makes me feel very privileged for I have always had a close attachment to the 1946 Lions. Childhood memories of bedtime rugby stories in the Foster household come flooding back as I recall so vividly my father, Trevor's all-time favourite, his adventures on the famous 1946 Indomitables tour to Australia and New Zealand.

He always reminded us proudly that this team became the only Lions to remain undefeated in a full Ashes series down under. The comradeship and bonding among the party must have been extraordinary as this tour above all others proved a real test of character and endurance.

What an adventure, over five months away from home, including 60 days at sea on a voyage around the world covering over 25,000 nautical miles. The outward journey on the HMS Indomitable an aircraft carrier was eventful. Remarkably the Indomitable's slogan was "Fighting Through", a fitting war cry for the Lions.

Colourful images were painted in his stories of the amazing encounter with the infamous Captain Neptune as they reached the equator. The many hours spent on the ship's decks playing hockey, tennis, touch rugby and basketball with the ship's crew to improve fitness levels and relieve the boredom. The return voyage also had its moments he recalled when the players watched in horror as lightening struck their ship, the R.M.S. Rangitiki, and the interminable rolling of the vessel often fogbound across the unforgiving Atlantic.

My mind created pictures of the enthusiastic flag waving Australian crowd which welcomed the team as they finally arrived in Sydney after a most uncomfortable final 2,600 mile overland train journey from Perth. The marvellous reception gave a measure of the importance of this tour to a sport starved nation and made a lasting impression on me.

We were told about the great players and personalities on the tour, especially the revered captain Gus Risman and always when asked my father's choice as his all-time great player. "Gus showed such composure in the heat of the battle and was our inspirational leader throughout the tour" he used to say.

The mighty bulldozing prop Frank Whitcombe, a close family friend, who at over 17 stone put the fear of God into the Australians. Then there was Joe Egan, the classiest of hookers, whose pace and guile around the field was a big factor in the test victories.

Trevor would gush over his Welsh back row-colleagues, Ike Owens "the best attacking forward on the tour", Doug Phillips whom the legendary Arthur Clues held in such high esteem as that big rough Welshman who never took a backward step and also Les White of York: "A pacy natural athlete who moved so quickly away from the overcrowded scrimmaging".

Another great player was Willie Horne, who was recognised as a most gifted footballer with the skills and magic to split defences with his quicksilver passing. The Australian crowds adored him.

My father though always had a kindly word for that larger than life character, tour journalist Eddie Waring, who became a loyal and respected friend to the players. "Nothing was ever too much for Eddie" Often sponge and bucket carrier on match days he also managed the tourists' popular Welsh players male voice choir, booking numerous engagements to swell the coffers.

There was no great entourage of physios, nutritionists, coaches or psychologists as back-up on this trip. It was mostly 'do-it-yourself' and it brought a determination and steel to the squad. Spirits were always high.

This was a tour of no little discomfort and some real adversity, particularly when it came to travel and accommodation. My father said that despite the many difficulties there was never any risk of a mutiny since all the players respected the management. They were all proud and honoured to be representing their country again so soon after many had served in overseas conflict with the armed forces during the war.

Certainly no quarter was given on the field of play. The tests both in Australia on the sun baked grounds and New Zealand in the deep mud were hard and uncompromising affairs. They often resulted in pitch battles between strong willed men at the peak of their physical prowess. Open and free flowing rugby was a rarity since there was obviously so much at stake, nevertheless there were some great tries scored and many lifelong friendships forged.

Fifty years on from those childhood memories and by some incredible coincidence I have recently met for the first time the son of Ike Owens, my father's room mate from that successful 1946 tour. Michael Owens and I were both attending, quite independently, the BBC *Antiques Roadshow* at Lords cricket ground in aid of Sport Relief. We had each taken memorabilia from the 'Indomitables' tour and were able to share stories and memories from our respective fathers.

One thing has led to another and we have now been contacted by several other close relatives of The Indomitables including those of Doug Phillips, Les White, Harry Murphy, Willie Davies, Bob Nicholson, Gus Risman and the two surviving tourists Joe Egan and Bryn Knowelden. Through these contacts additional tour archives have been uncovered including a diary written by Doug Phillips that has provided valuable material for this amazing book.

I have no doubt the book will provide a lasting legacy to those 26 men who became the famous rugby league "Indomitables" and the pride of the Lions. They will always be remembered as an important part of our game's great heritage.

**Simon Foster**
February 2009

Simon Foster lives in Beverley with his wife Nicola, daughter Hannah and son Michael. He is sports enthusiast, and has a passion for rugby league. He remembers first watching his father, Trevor Foster MBE, playing at Odsal in 1955. He has supported Bradford ever since. He is a qualified rugby league coach, and was one of the author's of *Trevor Foster – The life of a rugby league legend* which was published in 2005.

## About the author

Colin Thomson was born in Bradford and began a lifelong love affair with his home town club, after being taken to Odsal in the 1940s by an uncle who had played for Northern in their days at Birch Lane. These were heady days for Bradford Northern, with a team of stars assembled by the famous Harry Hornby. Many of the team were Welsh, as were many other league players. Bradford's most skilful player he recalls was W.H.T. Davies. Many writers mention his devastating speed, but this overlooks his true skills. His favourite ploy was to dummy opposing defences, and leave huge gaps for his colleagues to score.

Colin's only claim to rugby fame was going to the same school as Frank Whitcombe's two boys. Like all schoolboys league fans then he was fascinated by Eric Batten, who had his hair parted in the centre with a short back and side's haircut, and features carved in stone. His party trick was not to round defenders, but jump over them. In their schoolboy minds he could leap higher than an Olympic high jumper.

The 1946 tour raised many happy memories as a relative of Colin's worked for Cable and Wireless. They were responsible for relaying the latest price of wool to the Bradford Wool Exchange from Australia. At the end of the day's trading, they relayed results from any British sporting tours, and Australian football results for the pools companies during the football off season. For a youngster, this was rugby heaven, obtaining the latest news and scores before the press.

For the last 25 years he has lived in South Wales, working in the Health Service. His first year in the Principality saw the demise of the Blue Dragons rugby league team. Last year, in the Queen's Birthday Honours list, he was awarded the MBE, for raising thousands of pounds, mainly for RNIB Cymru, after running over 300 marathons all over the world. His wife Pat did the real hard work – not only arranging race entries, but organising the fundraising. The second half of his citation was for services to the National Health Service, through his involvement in clinical research. He is still heavily involved in this work, especially looking at accident and emergency services. He works closely with the medical schools of Cardiff, Swansea and Bangor Universities.

Being a researcher, and living in South Wales, he saw it as a logical progression to seek out the stories of former rugby league players who were raised in Bridgend. Ike Owens lived in the next street to Colin, and another local resident from the Indomitables tour was Arthur Bassett.

He was surprised to discover how many former players were war heroes. His schoolboy's memories a reserved school master, Bradford centre Jack Kitching, but in the war Kitching spent four hours floating in the icy cold waters of the Irish Sea after his ship was torpedoed. He then went straight on to serve in the Mediterranean on the heavily bombed Malta convoys.

This is Colin's first book about rugby league.

## Acknowledgements

Thanks to Simon Foster for writing the foreword, Michael O'Hare and Peter Lush for sub-editing, Steve McCarthy for designing the cover, Sherill the daughter of Doug Phillips and Simon Foster for permission to reproduce Doug Phillips's tour diary and to use photographs from his collection; Simon Foster, Mike Inman, Harry Edgar and *Rugby League Journal*, Bud Lisle and everyone else who supplied photographs or programme covers, the Rugby Football League for permission to reproduce photos from the Dai Jenkins collection, Robert Gate and Sean Fagan for help with the tour records, Michael Owens for giving me access to his father, Ike Owens's press cuttings, my wife Pat for so much help and support, Peter Lush and Dave Farrar for publishing the book and the staff of Biddles for printing it.

## England or Great Britain

Although the team that toured Australia is commonly called Great Britain, they played the matches under the banner of England, despite almost half the tourists being Welsh. In rugby league records, the appearances are regarded as being for Great Britain, although that title wasn't used officially until 1947. There was also an England team at this time, playing against Wales, France and later Other Nationalities.

To be historically correct, we have used England when referring to matches, and in the appendices. The reports, particularly in Australia, usually referred to England as well. In the text, we have used 'tourists' or 'Lions' wherever possible.

## Currency

The currency used in Great Britain, Australia and New Zealand was the imperial Pounds, Shillings and Pence. There were 12 pence to a shilling, and 20 shillings to a pound. A shilling, in modern decimal terms, was 5p. Naturally, the currency was worth far more then than nowadays.

## Photographs

Most of the photos in this book are from private collections, in particular those of Doug Phillips (shown DP) and Dai Jenkins (shown RFL/ DJ), unless otherwise indicated. No copyright has been intentionally breached, please contact London League Publications Ltd if you believe there has been a breach of copyright. The photographs are over 60 years old, and some are not of a high quality, but we felt it was better to use them, accepting the limitations on their quality.

# Contents

## 1946 Lions tour reunion

On Sunday 15 March 2009, Simon Foster and Michael Owens organised a reunion of players and relatives from the 1946 tour. Joe Egan and Bryn Knowelden, the last two players still alive, along with many players' relatives were welcomed to The George Hotel and Gillette Rugby League Heritage Centre by Mike Stephenson and Sam Morton. It was a memorable and moving occasion.

Bev Risman, Joe Egan, Mike Stephenson and Bryn Knowelden outside
The George Hotel. Bev Risman (Gus Risman's son) and Mike Stephenson
were both capped by Great Britain during their rugby league careers.
(Photo: Peter Lush)

Cartoon courtesy Gillette Rugby League Heritage Centre

# 1. Preparing for the tour

On Saturday 20 July 1946, England beat Australia 20–7 at the Sydney Cricket Ground to win the Ashes 2–0, and become the first British side to be unbeaten in an Ashes series. Tries from Arthur Basset – who scored twice – George Curran and Ike Owens, three goals by Gus Risman and one by Ernest Ward, gave England a clear victory.

However, this tour was about much more than the test matches. It re-established international rugby league after the Second World War. The British players had overcome great hardships in their trip to Australia. Ian Heads and David Middleton say in their centenary history of the game in Australia that "Australian rugby league hosted a tour by England in 1946, when such an event seemed impossible in the disarray of the post-war world…"

\*\*\*\*\*

Life in Britain following the Second World War was very far from a land fit for heroes. After more than five years of war and its long working hours, limited leisure activities, bomb damage and the blandest diet imaginable, there was a general feeling of exhaustion. More than a third of the country's housing had no hot water, or for that matter a bath. Even if people could afford new clothing there was still the obstacle of having enough clothing ration coupons, and everyday essentials were harder to obtain than during the war. Queues outside bakers' shops started in the early morning, and the majority of public houses had a board outside declaring that they were sorry, but they had no beer. Added to this was the common rider, that they had no cigarettes either.

The public must have been confused what winning a war was all about, because they were now faced with even more restrictive food rationing, which was due in part to a dispute with the United States over 'lend lease'. This involved an accusation that some people in Britain had made fraudulent use of this scheme whereby a large number of products from America had been imported into Britain on the premise that they could be paid for later. Meat was a limited item in Britain, and one of these imported items was spam, which had become a luxury in Britain, usually served for Sunday tea. The cost of victory had been huge, and Britain was virtually bankrupt, all of which had led to a rise in prices, because of the shortage of manufactured goods. Of course there were still a number of people who played the system. Scarce goods could be bought on the black market, with no questions asked.

For the general public peace had bought little change. The major differences from wartime life were to have the street lighting switched

1

on, to hear the sound of church bells on Sundays, and to have loved ones return home, although many were still in uniform due to military needs following the war.

However, several items of food, including fruit from overseas, were now slowly reappearing in the shops. Despite the shortages, proud fathers still managed to fund their daughters' weddings which, following demobilisation, were becoming increasingly prolific. With so many men returning home there was also the start of a huge baby boom, and there appeared to be prams and pushchairs everywhere. Queuing, which had been a feature of wartime Britain, had altered very little though. Many necessary items would require long hours of waiting before they could be purchased. And new millionaires began to appear, their fortunes made mainly by buying and selling war surplus, or by land grabbers buying bomb sites, and selling them at a profit before payment was due.

## Sport and rugby league

In order to forget the shortages and the dreariness of life the public welcomed the reappearance of fully competitive sport, or watched the latest film emanating from the Hollywood studios, which introduced an element of glamour. One wartime benefit was that cinemas were now permanently open on Sundays, a move the government had introduced during the war to allow shift workers to see the films. Despite the fact that most of the sports grounds around the country were badly in need of attention, it did not stop the public from attending in great numbers to watch and support their local sides. The giant Odsal Stadium in Bradford was home to an ever increasing number of supporters, and rugby league was on a wave of popularity, as were most spectator sports.

Despite all these problems, and the fact that many people had not yet been discharged from the military services, and many sports grounds were as yet unavailable, sport was slowly returning to its pre-war level. The end of the war had been marked by a number of victory internationals, which comprised teams of international squads of players from all the serving forces playing exhibition matches. These games had been mainly played in football and both codes of rugby. Although only pride was at stake the attendances were huge.

In rugby league, a War Emergency League and the Challenge Cup had been played between 1939 and 1945. The Rugby League Council followed a missive from the Ministry of Labour to provide as much sport as possible to provide rest and relaxation for the workers. This was despite the fact that many of the male population were absent serving their country. A lack of playing areas was another major problem. Many of the main grounds were used as military bases,

2

including the likes of Wigan, Salford and Swinton. Crowd sizes for all matches were limited because of air raid restrictions. A match between Hull and Batley was abandoned because of an air raid. Clothes rationing meant that acquiring club shirts was very difficult. Sixteen clothing coupons were required for a set of kit, and clubs had to rely on players or supporters giving coupons from their own allowance. However, in September 1944, the RFL was given 870 coupons by the Board of Trade, as well as a quota of footballs and bladders.

Dewsbury, under the management of Eddie Waring, made use of professional players based at a local large military camp, enabling his home town club to reach a wartime Challenge Cup Final in 1943, when they beat Leeds 16–15 over two legs. Players he used as guests included Gus Risman, George Curran and Roy Francis and the team which played in the Challenge Cup Final included eight guests.

Towards the end of the war, there were two matches between rugby league and rugby union sides, under union rules and comprised of armed forces personnel. These had been so successful that a number of requests were made – and not only from league supporters – to make these an annual event. Sadly, there were going to be no further attempts to heal the breach between the codes. Despite the fact that many of the players had fought and played together, come peacetime they would be separated forever. Among letters belonging to Ike Owens, a player who regularly played both codes during the war, is a sad missive from the chaplain of the combined forces rugby union side. They had struck up a close friendship, and the chaplain wrote how much he regretted that with Ike playing rugby league regularly they would be unable to meet again, and how much he would miss their conversations together.

**1945–46**

The 1945–46 season had seen something like normality returning to the game of rugby league, and this despite the fact that not all players had finished their military service. Notwithstanding all the problems which existed, a full playing programme was completed, with the first post- war Challenge Cup Final being a close-run affair. Wakefield Trinity narrowly beat Wigan 13–12. A crowd of 54,730 at Wembley paid record receipts. With the restricted travelling provisions still in place this was an excellent attendance. During the season Bradford Northern had beaten Trinity 5–2 in the Yorkshire Cup Final. Wigan had also lost in the Final of the Lancashire Cup, Widnes beating them 7–3. However, Wigan did experience the joy of winning a final, taking the Championship by beating Huddersfield 13–4 at Maine Road, with 67,136 fans present.

The Lions touring party had already left for Australia on 3 April, which meant they missed both the Challenge Cup and Championship Finals, which were on 4 May and 18 May respectively.

The climate in Australia following the end of the Second World War was very much one of feeling isolated from Britain. Previously there had been very close ties with Britain and most of the population regarded it as their mother country. This feeling of isolation was without doubt, due to the threat of invasion from Japan during the war. The Japanese had made a determined assault to enlarge their Empire in the Antipodes, and as part of that aimed to invade Australia. For the first time in her history, Australia had been bombed, by the Japanese air force, at Port Moresby in Northern Australia (now Papua New Guinea). Also, Sydney harbour in 1942 had come under attack from miniature Japanese submarines. Certainly, without the assistance of the United States, the Japanese fighting machine would probably have prevailed. Britain had been in no position to give assistance, and following the embarrassing defeats in Singapore and Malaya, they had kept only a tenuous hold in that part of the world.

Australia itself was going through changes which had to be addressed. There was a general feeling of unrest in the country. A major problem which had arisen concerned working conditions. As in Britain, with many men of working age serving in the forces, women had been required to carry out their work in industry and transport. Unfortunately, the women had been paid at much lower rates than the men and employers were reluctant to pay returning men higher rates. Certainly this caused a lot of resentment and led to innumerable strikes across the continent, badly affecting transport which already faced shortages and fuel rationing.

Sport had been restricted due to a lack of young men, and had continued mainly in areas where men had been required for essential services such as mining and heavy industry. As in Britain, rugby league had continued, although there were no interstate matches after 1941. There were league competitions in Sydney and Brisbane.

The only visitors to Australian shores had been American troops and General McCarthy had made Australia a base for his command during the years before his return to the Philippines. The country needed to develop again, and required a dramatic rise in immigrants. It also missed international sport, although some Australian forces teams had played in Great Britain.

### The Indomitables are born

The Australian federal minister for external affairs, Dr Herbert Evatt, who was also a patron of the New South Wales rugby league and would later become leader of the Australian Labor Party, came to Britain in the September of 1945, to establish the feasibility of a British sporting tour of Australia in 1946, and to once again reinforce that special bond which had always existed between the two nations. The only British sporting body which appeared to be prepared to make the tour possible, and was willing to overcome the obstacles of a major tour, was the Rugby Football League. Certainly the cricket and rugby union bodies felt that they were in no position to contemplate such an undertaking.

The possibility of staging such a tour so quickly and following a major world war even today would be very unlikely. Both nations had serious fuel problems and manpower shortages – 20 per cent of the male population had been called up for military service, and many were still waiting to be discharged. Even today it is doubtful if modern players would be ready to play 19 matches on the other side of the world, including a three test series, then tour New Zealand, playing another test and six other games. The seas journey itself took four weeks from Great Britain, and the same time to return. This was in a world which had hardly started to recover from the war.

Also, a number of players had been away from home for six years, many had served overseas, and so it would place a great strain on their family life. The other factor, which at the time appeared to have been overlooked, was to ensure that every player who was selected would actually be available. Many of the clubs in the 1945–46 season still had players unavailable because of military commitments, and due to the country's more pressing needs, very few younger players had been given much opportunity to develop and play the game.

Given the very serious problems such a tour would create, it is not surprising that the Rugby League Council initially deferred making a decision. It is all the more remarkable that they were not long in coming to it. On 24 October 1945 the Council voted to go ahead with a tour in the following spring, by the clear majority of 19 votes to four.

This was to be the first major sporting tour undertaken by a British sporting body since before the war, and presumably the Rugby League Council was putting much faith in the support of the Australian Government. The Council has often criticised for not making decisions, but certainly here this was not the case.

At the beginning of 1946 there was still no transport arranged, and already the project was starting to appear doomed. The Australian High Commission in London, in a letter to the Rugby League Council, underlined how difficult it was to give priority to a sporting side when many thousands of Australian servicemen were still awaiting transport home. Although this major difficulty was not resolved, the Council still pressed on with the arrangements. The touring party was to be selected on 11 March, and then be ready to sail on 1 April 1946. Less than two weeks before the planned departure date a passage was secured on the Australian aircraft carrier HMS Indomitable on 3 April.

5

In such ways are great sporting names born. The tourists were about to earn their new enduring title which is now a rugby league legend.

Selection for the tour was not easy and players' records as well as recent performances had to be taken into consideration. The selectors had been able to watch England and Wales play two international matches during the 1945–46 season, which enabled them to have the opportunity to assess many new players who were making their way into the game, plus those who had recently joined the professional ranks from rugby union. The first international match was at Swansea in November, when a Wales side captained by Willie Davies of Bradford Northern beat England 11–3. This match was watched by 30,000 spectators, including American servicemen. This figure still stands as an attendance record at the St Helens ground in Swansea. It was a wonderful homecoming for Willie Davies, who was made captain for the game, and was his first match there since moving to rugby league from Swansea and joining Bradford.

On 6 January 1946, a British Rugby League XIII had played a French XIII at Parc des Princes in Paris. The British side had a convincing win, 19–6. Then on 23 February, England beat France 16–6 at Swinton, with Albert Johnson scoring a hat-trick of tries for England.

Surprisingly, despite the pressures which would be put on family life, very few players made themselves unavailable to tour, and those that did were mainly the victims of injuries.

As well as the international matches, two tour trials were staged, one at Wigan and the other at Headingley. In the first the 'colours' beat the 'whites' 18–3, while in the second, the 'whites' won 18–14. However, the international between England and France at Swinton was three days after the Leeds game, so the English players selected for the international missed the trial.

There was still one major obstacle to get over, and that was that three of the players who had been selected were still serving in the armed forces: Bradford's Ernest Ward, Les White of York, and Doug Phillips of Oldham. The officials of the Rugby League Council asked the Yorkshire MPs to use parliamentary pressure to secure their release in time for the tourists' embarkation in the HMS Indomitable from Plymouth Devonport docks on Wednesday 3 April 1946. Replacements were available, but all three players joined the tourists.

The Barrow contingent – Willie Horne, Jim Lewthwaite, Joe Jones and Bryn Knowelden, along with Workington Town's Fred Hughes and tour manager Wilf Gabbatt were seen off from Barrow station on 1 April by 100 supporters. They spent the evening in London, and then travelled down to Plymouth.

The players were to be paid 30 shillings a week (British currency - £1.50 today) while at sea, and 50 shillings a week on land ('Colonial' currency – £2.50 today). The wives of married men were paid £3 per

6

week, and there was an allowance of seven shillings and sixpence per child. Also, the players would receive a third of the tour profits split between them.

The players through their contract for the tour agreed to:

(a) Complete the tour and return to England;

(b) Obey and fulfil every order given by the managers or either of them;

(c) Act in the capacity of checkers if and when required;

(d) Act as trainers when not required to play and generally to assist the managers in every possible way to the best of their skill and ability;

(e) To be responsible for all jerseys and other football outfit provided by and to be regarded as the property of the Council and under no circumstances to give any jersey away; and

(f) Behave themselves in a gentlemanly way both on and off the field and to take every precaution to prevent themselves from losing form and to make every effort by judicious training to retain their form and to make the tout a success from a playing point of view.

The players had a squad numbering system for their shirts – maybe to make it easier to investigate if one was damaged or given away. It is also interesting to note that the players were required to return to England. The international transfer ban between Great Britain and Australia had lapsed, and this was an issue that arose during the tour.

Doug Phillips and George Curran at the Gaffin Hotel in Leeds
when signing on for the tour. (DP)

Gus Risman with the Australian High Commissioner before the tour. (RFL)

# 2. The players

Thirteen clubs were represented in the touring party. Bradford Northern had six players, Wigan and Barrow four apiece, Leeds two, and Halifax, Huddersfield, Oldham, Wakefield Trinity, Warrington, Widnes and York one each. There was criticism of some of the selectors' choices. It was particularly strange that only 11 forwards were chosen in the party of 26 players. This meant that the workhorses of the touring party would regularly have to play two matches a week. It appeared that the possibility of injuries to players had not been fully considered, although the general opinion was that given the time schedule, then this was probably the best side that could be assembled.

There could be no criticism of the choice of captain and vice-captain, Gus Risman and Tommy McCue. They were both recognised as two of the most outstanding players of the age, and were the only two with previous experience of a Lions tour. Welshman Risman, who incidentally was born and bred in the Cardiff dock area known as Tiger Bay which would later produce such notables as Billy Boston, Johnny Freeman and Colin Dixon, was captain. He was still a veritable giant with Salford, having also had plenty of pre-war international experience. Importantly, he was a very good diplomat, which would no doubt be a key factor on a tour of Australia. However, at 36 years of age, it could be said that he was a little old for international rugby, although there had been few signs of any deterioration in his general play. Many players who were playing then rated Gus as the most complete rugby player they had ever played with or against.

The vice-captain, Tommy McCue, was the same age, and certainly the Australians recognised him as the world's outstanding scrum-half. Besides having outstanding ball distribution, he was an exceptionally skilled ball-kicker who had very often broken the heart of many opposing sides by his astute place kicking. Even the Australians, who do not give bouquets very often, especially to British opponents, acknowledged that the Widnes player was an undoubted match-winner. Allied to his passing and kicking skills was his inborn talent of selling dummies to opponents. Many defenders who he had faced were only too ready to acknowledge this talent.

The two full-backs were Joe Jones of Barrow and Wigan's Martin Ryan. Jones was seen as the first choice for this position, and while a number of others were considered, it was felt that the majority of outstanding full-backs in the game had seen their best days. At 22 years of age, Ryan was the baby of the party. During the first season following the war he had shown the necessary qualities to become an outstanding attacking full-back. Certainly the selectors believed that the tour would show his full potential. It must have been a close call between Ryan and Dewsbury's Jimmy Ledgard. Ledgard had played in both the trial matches, and was the top goalkicker in British rugby league in 1945–46, with 88 goals. These two players throughout their careers competed for the full-back spot in internationals.

Injuries hit both full-backs on the tour, and subsequently both had the misfortune to play little part in it. However, hindsight is a wonderful thing. The selectors' decision to put their faith in the promise of Martin Ryan was to be well rewarded in future years.

Incidentally, this was one of the oldest touring parties on record, with eight of the team being over 30, and another three were 29 years old. The war was clearly a limiting factor in the development of young players, and this is reflected in the selection of the touring party. Some of the players were also war-time converts from rugby union, and lacked substantial top class rugby league experience.

In addition National Service was still in operation, and certainly this was another hurdle which had a major role in preventing the selection of younger players. Almost every young man had to do military service, unless they were working in industries essential for the war effort, such as mining or engineering.

As always, the selectors had no problems in having outstanding players for the wing positions. Indeed, they could afford to ignore the claims of such as Alan Edwards who had scored the defining try for Salford in the 1939 Championship Final, and who had been a success in Australia on the 1936 tour. The two first choices for the team were Eric Batten of Bradford, who had been the leading try scorer in British rugby league for the last two seasons and the excellent defensive player from Warrington, Albert Johnson. The latter was not the fastest of wingers, but any lack of speed was amply compensated for by a superb body swerve which left many defenders completely stranded. Johnson was to take without complaint any amount of thuggish tackling from the Australians, and come back for more.

The other two wingers selected were Welshman Arthur Bassett, a big powerful player who had already played for Wales at rugby union, and had been a major star in that sphere. He had joined Halifax in 1939, for a signing-on fee of £999. This unusual figure was due to one of the Halifax directors having a bet that they could sign him for less than £1,000. Bassett was given the extra pound out of club funds. His debut appearance with the reserve side attracted more than 5,000 spectators. He had been a major factor in that club winning the Challenge Cup in 1939.

Due to the excitement of the Halifax cup run nobody had ensured he could continue his role as a policeman with one of the West Riding Police Forces, and he had then taken an appointment with the Derbyshire police, and played union most weekends for Nottingham during the war years. Incidentally, he remained with that police force after the war, and travelled to Halifax to play until 1948, when he finally transferred to York to ease travelling, surprisingly then playing in the position of loose-forward. On retirement he became security officer for Chatsworth House, and settled in Derbyshire for his remaining years.

The fourth winger was Barrow's Jim Lewthwaite. Although he did not figure in the test arena on this tour, he scored many tries against the country teams, and became a Cumbrian legend during his playing career. Incidentally, he and Eric Batten were always in contention throughout the tour as the leading try scorers. Their career records covered a similar length of time, and both figure in the chart for leading try scorers of all time, Batten scoring 443 and Lewthwaite 383

The centres were all outstanding, and injuries not withstanding, were bound to cause the tour selection panel future problems. One of them, Ernest Ward of Bradford, had another talent, goalkicking, and he was an excellent understudy to Gus Risman, who was a superb marksman. Ward became one of the top players in the game, and it is hardly surprising he returned to Australia and New Zealand in 1950 as the Lions tour captain. Ward was tall and very athletic, good both in defence and attack, and he and Trevor Foster were to become two of Bradford's greatest ever players. Ward had signed for Bradford as a 16 year old in 1936.

Ted Ward had joined Wigan in 1938, having played union for Llanelli. He had been seen as a rising star in Welsh rugby union. That doyen of contemporary rugby league reporters, Harry Sunderland, intimated that the new Welsh crop of players fell below the level of those of pre-war, but during the tour changed his mind dramatically about Ted. He was rather the dark horse of the tour with obviously hidden talents, because he took on the Wigan goalkicking role on his return from the tour, and in the 1947–48 and 1948–49 seasons, not only led the rugby league goalkicking charts, but was also the leading aggregate points scorer.

One of the other two centres was Jack Kitching, a big strong-running centre from Bradford, who because of his baldness looked much older than his 25 years. He would soon be embroiled in one of the most notorious rugby league incidents of all time. Barrow's Bryn Knowelden, an excellent accomplished player who perhaps just lacked the top skills of his contemporaries but was certainly good enough to win his one and only international cap, was the fourth centre.

The Lions in former years had always been renowned for outstanding half-backs, and the best of 1946 was certainly no less inferior. The real question was who would partner Tommy McCue. The choice was between Leeds's Dai Jenkins and Barrow's Willie Horne. Incidentally, Willie Horne was also a professional cricketer, very rare

11

among rugby league players. He was for a time on the Lancashire County Cricket ground staff. Bradford's Willie Davies had the unenviable task of understudying McCue.

If there was competition for the stand-off position, there was an almost identical situation for the hooker slot. Wigan's Joe Egan and George Curran of Salford were in contention. At this time when the ball went straight into the scrum between the packs, the hooker had to rely on his props to secure a successful strike. Both Egan and Curran were real ball winners from a scrum, and the edge was probably towards Egan, in having his club colleague Ken Gee as a certain selection prop in the forthcoming tests. Curran did have one advantage over Joe Egan in that he was also an outstanding prop, and excelled in the loose play around the scrums. This was a useful asset if there was a shortage of forwards. Later Joe Egan also showed in a country game that he was an outstanding second-rower.

Beside Joe Egan in the pack, an almost certain choice for prop was the giant Welshman, Frank Whitcombe of Bradford, who regularly weighed in just short of 18 stone. Despite this, he was surprisingly light on his feet. Off the field Frank was the most affable of men, but was not averse to making sure that an opponent knew he was in charge when he tackled someone.

One of his favourite ploys was to grasp an opponent round the waist then lift him over his head, and drop him head-first behind him. Modern-day referees would not take kindly to this type of tackling. The other main prop was Fred Hughes of Workington, better known today as the father of Emlyn, a legendry player with Liverpool Football Club and England. Fred was very much the workhorse of the props. It was almost unknown for him to score a try, but he could power his way out of defence with hard, head-down running for the whole 80 minutes of a match. He was suffering from gout when the tour got underway, something he kept well hidden from the Australians.

The second-row forwards were all strong and powerful with good pace. Harry Murphy, aged 24, was a promising player with Wakefield, who regularly played at loose-forward for his club. However, he would have to wait until 1950 for his only test cap. York's Les White was one of the major successes on the tour while Huddersfield's Bob Nicholson was to star in a fearsome pack with his club in the post-war years. Oldham's Doug Phillips, at 26, was a big, strong running forward, who certainly knew how to tackle, and perhaps was the main surprise selection of the tour. He first played for Oldham in February 1945, and after only seven games for the club he was selected for the tour. He had joined Oldham from Swansea rugby union towards the end of the war. Until the departure of the tour party he had not yet scored a try in rugby league.

These players were youngsters by this tour's age standards, and who were now having the opportunity of making a name for themselves, and make up for the years they had lost to the war.

The other second-rower was Trevor Foster a big, fast-running Welshman, who could score tries given the slightest opportunity. Trevor had been a regular selection in wartime rugby league internationals, playing for Wales and the Combined Services representative sides.

The final player in the party was a 27 year old Welshman, Leeds's Ike Owens. He had been regularly selected for wartime internationals and the victory internationals in 1945. Most of these had been rugby union matches, and he was somewhat of an unknown in rugby league circles. He had signed for Leeds in 1943, but had been given little opportunity because of war service to play for the club. Ike had the misfortune not to have won a peacetime Wales rugby union cap. In 1939 he had been outstanding in the Welsh rugby union trials, and while he played for Wales in the home internationals early in 1940 they did not count as full internationals. Owens was also a war hero, having been awarded the Air Force Flying Medal for Gallantry, one of the very few non-aircrew personnel to achieve this award. He did not get his medal easily. He made 198 recorded parachute jumps, and had been on 16 missions over enemy occupied Europe. In an interview with an Australian reporter he remarked that when he completed 360 jumps he had stopped counting.

Those who had seen him play rated him as possibly the British squad's new secret weapon. With his amazing acceleration he expected to flourish on the firmer grounds in Australia.

The full squad with their shirt numbers was:

| | | | |
|---|---|---|---|
| 1. | Martin Ryan | 14. | Tommy McCue |
| 2. | Joe Jones | 15. | Dai Jenkins |
| 3. | Eric Batten | 16. | Frank Whitcombe |
| 4. | Joe Lewthwaite | 17. | Fred Hughes |
| 5. | Gus Risman | 18. | Ken Gee |
| 6. | Ernest Ward | 19. | Joe Egan |
| 7. | Ted Ward | 20. | George Curran |
| 8. | Bryn Knowelden | 21. | Bob Nicholson |
| 9. | Jack Kitching | 22. | Doug Phillips |
| 10. | Arthur Bassett | 23. | Les White |
| 11. | Albert Johnson | 24. | Trevor Foster |
| 12. | Willie Horne | 25. | Harry Murphy |
| 13. | Willie Davies | 26. | Ike Owens |

The tour managers were Walter Popplewell, of Batley who had previous experience of the role, as he had been the tour manager on the 1936 tour. The business manager was Wilf Gabbatt of Barrow. Both men had formerly been chairmen of the Rugby League Council. Popplewell was responsible for the playing and selection part of the tour. Hull KR's representative on the Rugby League Council, Walter Crockford, was on the tour as a paying guest, although he was often involved in meetings with the Australian and New Zealand rugby league authorities.

This was the first time that a tour was undertaken with a press entourage. Two very famous reporters who covered the tour were Harry Sunderland, an Australian by birth, and Eddie Waring, who would become the game's first big television personality. Eddie was a very sociable man and was well known for talking in club bars after matches to officials and players alike. Readers of his column in the *Sunday Pictorial* knew Eddie always wanted to be first with a scoop.

Harry Sunderland would meet the party in Australia, but Eddie Waring, Ernest Crawthorne of the *Manchester Evening News* and *Yorkshire Post* reporter Alfred Drewry accompanied the tourists on the cruise to Australia, the very first time such an event had occurred.

# 3. The voyage

The HMS Indomitable, which only 12 months previously had suffered severe damage from a kamikaze attack during the invasion of Hiroshima, embarked on 3 April. It was not lost on the Barrow players that while the aircraft carrier was part of the Australian Navy, she had actually been built in the Barrow shipyards. Eddie Waring wrote in the *Sunday Pictorial* in his usual stirring manner that "Two tons of Britain's rugby league footballers are now added to the 23,000 tons of the famous aircraft-carrier Indomitable." He also said that Lewthwaite, Horne and Knowelden had even helped to build the ship, but "didn't know about it".

The majority of the 2,000 passengers were returning Australian servicemen. And if any of the party had religious worries these could be resolved by a party of six Irish priests.

Some players did not take well to the sea voyage. Bob Nicholson recalled in his testimonial brochure that he suffered badly from seasickness on the trip. In his first report from the ship, Eddie Waring said that "Lewthwaite ran faster than he has ever done at Craven Park to visit the Bay of Biscay to be sick, followed closely by Horne." Waring admits that he came third in this race. Nicholson had got used to life on board, and been given his certificate for crossing the equator, when the last three days going into Australia were very rough and his problems returned.

In *Rugby Renegade* Gus Risman recalls that the tourists were put on the crew list as Petty Officers, and given the privileges for this rank. This included their own bunks and use of the Petty Officers' mess. He says that he was allocated more space, probably because he was the captain, but others were less fortunate, being given berths near the engine rooms. Frank Whitcombe was one of the unlucky ones, and woke up every day covered in sweat. The tourists jokingly told him that a Turkish bath each night would keep his weight down.

Training only started in the second half of the voyage. Trevor Foster was put in charge by Gus Risman and the tour managers. Trevor recalled in his biography: "It was my job to get the players up at seven in the morning, lead the PE sessions and run the lads round the boat until breakfast time. Getting people like Frank Whitcombe up wasn't much fun sometimes, I can tell you, although they all did take it in good part really. Frank and Ken Gee, our two big props, were quite ill at ease in those hot conditions and they weren't keen on running around. It seemed to affect them badly, probably because of their size. They would try to find a cool, shady corner to hide, where they could sit down and relax, hoping to get their breathing back to normal." However, Trevor didn't always take his large colleague so

15

seriously, commenting to Eddie Waring that Whitcombe had been allocated a cabin near the flight deck "because they were frightened his 17 stone would sink the ship".

A canvas swimming pool was very popular with the tourists, and they were able to utilise an empty hangar to play basketball. However, the most popular sport on board was seven-a-side deck hockey. Most of the passengers participated in a knockout competition. The eventual winners were a tough side of naval stokers who, in the semi-final had a close win over a side called the 'sky pilots' mainly made up of the Irish priests. Almost 50 years before Super League was born, the Wigan players adopted the name Wigan Warriors as their team title for deck hockey. Doug Phillips got a cut lip in one game, and had two teeth loosened.

Another popular activity was 'hand football'. The Lions could have lost one of their players through this game. Trevor Foster recalls that the ball flew into the Red Sea, 60 feet below the deck. Eric Batten jumped into the water to retrieve the ball. When he returned, the captain told him off and said he was lucky still to be alive – the water was infested with sharks.

The voyage took four weeks, including passing through the Suez Canal. It took eight hours to navigate its 100-mile length. There were stops at Gibraltar, where Eddie Waring was able to go ashore and bring back orange for the tourists, Malta, Aden (now known as Yemen) where the Crown Prince brought gifts of fruit and coffee in thanks for the troops' war efforts. The final stop was at Colombo, the capital of Ceylon, now known as Sri Lanka. Some passengers left the ship at Malta and Colombo. They finally docked at Fremantle in Western Australia.

The players were able to go ashore at Malta, Aden and Colombo. Doug Phillips wrote in his diary how shocked he was by conditions in Aden.

The regular workouts meant that the players arrived in the peak of condition. Before their final departure from the aircraft carrier, The Indomitable's Captain Andrews asked the tourists if they would play an exhibition match for the crew and the local people. This they were more than willing to do, and it was agreed that all the money raised would be given to naval charities as a thank-you to the ship's crew.

The match took place on 30 April with the tourists splitting up into two sides: McCue's Reds and Risman's Blues. The Reds won 24–5. Johnson, with two, Ted Ward, Phillips, Lewthwaite and Ernest Ward scored tries for the Reds, with Ernest Ward, Ted Ward and Horne all kicking goals. The Blues' points came from an Owens try and Risman goal. The match was attended by the Mayor of Fremantle, who responded by arranging for all the party to attend a civic dinner after the match, and a formal reception. Eddie Waring refereed the match.

16

It was well attended. A collection taken at the ground raised £44. The Rugby Football League augmented this with a 10 guinea donation.

Arrangements had been made for the tourists to complete the final leg of their journey by sailing on the aircraft carrier Victorious to Sydney, which would be their base for the most of the tour. Unfortunately, the ship had been involved in a violent tropical storm which caused it to require substantial repairs, making it impossible for her to sail for at least three weeks.

It was then decided that the party would cross the Australian continent by rail, although berths could not be booked on a troop train before 7 May, and so the party had to stay at a military camp. Meanwhile, as the Indomitable had to fulfil other duties, she sailed away from Australia. The tour managers had tried to arrange for the party to fly from Freemantle to Sydney, but were unable to do this.

Berths is a somewhat grandiose description of the train's sleeping quarters, which meant that four or five players were required to share one berth. This final leg of the journey was 2,600 miles, and was scheduled to take five days and nights. However, another delay at Perth added an extra 24 hours to the journey. On two nights there was no sleeping accommodation at all, and the players either slept on the floor or sitting up. Wilf Gabbatt commented that "The conditions to Melbourne were certainly grim and considerable discomfort and inconvenience were experienced by all." However, from Melbourne to Sydney, the last leg of the trip, sleeping cars were provided.

There was no restaurant car on the train. Meals were served on the railway track from boilers and eaten by the party either sitting on the railway lines or anywhere they could make a seat. Around Adelaide meals were provided in canteens, but flies were a nuisance.

The food was "fairly good in quality but lacking in quantity" according to Wilf Gabbatt's official tour report. The party had to buy extra on the journey. The tour management did give out extra money to cover this. The players' compartments were inspected every morning by a duty officer, this being a troop train, and they were commended for the cleanliness of their accommodation. Rugby league historian Tom Webb wrote that "The commanding officer issued instructions that the team must wash the floors of their carriage. This was so unreasonable that Wilfred Gabbatt, rather than ask the players to perform this task, went down on his knees and scrubbed them himself."

The Lions arrived in Sydney on 12 May, over five weeks after they had left Plymouth. They were met by members of the Australian Rugby League Board of Control and the New South Wales League. However, no transport had been arranged for them, and the party had to get their own taxies, and pay their own fares, to the hotel.

In his biography of Willie Horne, Mike Gardner describes the players as "aching, exhausted and relieved, looking more like bearded, emaciated convicts than professional rugby league players".

In Sydney, they stayed in the Olympic Hotel, near the Sydney Cricket Ground. However, the accommodation was so cramped that the party considered moving. Trevor Foster recalled that the hotel was in an area frequented by prostitutes, and was certainly not in a smart area of Sydney. On the other hand, he said there was a Catholic church for players of that faith, and the training facilities were nearby.

Having settled in Sydney, the players were delighted at the number of social invitations they received, which continued during the tour.

Unfortunately, problems with accommodation and transport were not an isolated occurrence on the forthcoming tour. All too often members of the party were left to make their own travel arrangements. Eddie Waring later said that no international touring party had travelled so frugally as the 1946 squad did.

On their arrival, the players very soon found out that any complaint would be treated as a slight against Australian hospitality. They were expected to go along with everything that was arranged. One of the players happened to complain to a reporter about the length of time the journey had taken. This remark created instant umbrage with the Australian public who, after reading a somewhat biased report, indicated that the sportsmen were fortunate to have transport to travel, when there were good Australian boys who had served their country were still waiting to get home to their loved ones. In these days of hi-tech communications, it is very difficult to realise how hard it was to communicate with Britain or, for that matter, across the continent of Australia itself.

In 1946, most sporting reports were sent by cable to Bradford, which was the centre of the wool trading industry, and a very essential part of both British and Australian economies. Someone who worked for Cable and Wireless said at that time wool prices had first priority and after the wool market closed for the day, he was then allowed to pass on other items, such as the news, rugby and cricket reports.

He was a popular man in Bradford public houses thanks to having the latest sporting scores. Another important task he had was to forward the football results for the Australian pools service, and in the summer months he relayed the Australian football results, which the British betting companies such as Vernon's, and Littlewoods required for their summer football coupons.

## Touring schedule

The arrangements were very ad-hoc. The second match of the tour was played at the Australian Governor's residence in Canberra, and was not initially included in the official list of tour matches.

The tourists started the tour playing a warm up game against a Southern Districts in Junee, a remote country area in New South Wales, but following this, and unknown to the tourists, they would be involved in matches against tough opposition right up to the first test. What was worse was the fact that there was no rest period built into the programme. The two matches against New South Wales representative sides prior to the first test were bound to be hard with the Australian players giving their all in order to gain international selection.

There would be three test matches against Australia, with the first and third ones to be played in Sydney. For the middle part of the tour, the tourists moved to Queensland, with the second test being played in Brisbane. The final leg of the tour was still very sketchy to say the least, but would be in New Zealand, and include one test there. The tourists would have hundred of miles to travel, with very little rest between matches, and usually playing at least two games a week.

In all, 27 matches were played, with regular rail travel to the remoter parts of New South Wales and Queensland. It was an extremely punishing programme, and clearly undertaken without any prior consideration of the Australian government's restrictions on travel. It is a great pity that the British management of the party were unable to use air travel more.

But if anyone thought the tour would be a disaster, they need not have worried because the Australian public was weary of war, and the opportunity of watching a touring team from the old country was not to be missed. Reports of all the matches identify spectators falling from the roofs of stands, where they were attempting to get a better view. Some grandstands collapsed under the weight of too many watchers. Despite these calamities, there were no serious casualties, and everyone appeared to enjoy themselves immensely. Many families in the areas where the matches were to be played would find themselves host to long-lost relatives who would stay with them in order to be able to watch a match against the Lions.

The remote country areas really enjoyed these games, and invited the tourists into their homes for meals and homespun entertainment. It was ironic that the Australian government, having imposed severe travel restrictions, now saw throngs of travelling residents who were determined to see the tourists play. Very often the Australian roads became like a replay of the arrival of the early settlers, as horses once again became the basic form of transport, as any type of vehicle that could be utilised was put into commission.

England had not lost a test series against Australia since 1920. They were the favourites to win the series. However, the Australian press was saying that this present touring side lacked the flair of previous ones.

19

During the war, the Australian public had sent food parcels to Britain, and their troops had been an important part of the war effort. The famous Australian writer – and great rugby league fan – Thomas Keneally recalls that "The story may be apocryphal, but it is said that when the English team disembarked from their bus for a training session at the Sydney Cricket Ground, an Aussie bystander who saw the size of the British forwards Whitcombe and Gee shouted 'No more bloody bundles for Britain!' Whoever, it was, he was declaring that for rugby league for the world the war had ended, and all bets were off."

Even so, such was the hero worship of the Australian public for the tourists' celebrities that Trevor Foster recalls that Gus Risman, Ernest Ward, Eric Batten and Ike Owens were treated like royalty wherever they went. They were given the best tables in restaurants, and received the best service possible. Anything the tourists said about the game of rugby was treated with awe by the press and public alike.

Trevor also said that this time the Australian side were determined not to lose, and were equally determined to treat all three test matches as a war. He felt that they wouldn't concede victory until the final whistle sounded.

After so much travelling, and the innumerable delays, the tourists must have welcomed the comparative lack of intensity of that first week, and the opportunity to get their playing legs back to normal. Although their arrival in Sydney had been low key, it was not long before various celebrities were calling into their hotel to welcome the side to Australia. These included Fred Perry, the top British tennis player of the time, who was playing in an exhibition series, and the cast of *How Green Was My Valley.* This film, set in Wales and based on the book by Richard Llewellyn, had just been released in Australia, and was proving a worldwide hit. The film makers were doing a publicity launch in Sydney, and the publicity people were quick to home in on the Welsh members of the party. All these players were asked to comment on the film, and to participate with the cast of the film in photo shoots. While they may have been a little doubtful about the portrayal of Welsh life by the Hollywood studio, wisely they kept their views on this to themselves.

A number of receptions were held for the tourists. Despite the government's power restrictions which prohibited the use of buildings with excessive lighting being used for public functions, the locals were not to be deterred from providing the best of hospitality for them. They were taken on tours of the local sights in Sydney. Nothing was too much trouble and in fact they now found their social diaries filled to overflowing as everyone appeared to entertain them.

On 16 May the tourists were among a crowd of 27,866 who attended an interstate match at the Sydney Cricket Ground, where New South Wales beat Queensland 24–6. It was clear to the touring party that there were going to be problems with the interpretations of various rules. There were meetings of the tour management with their Australian counterparts, but the tour was plagued with what the Lions thought were strange refereeing decisions, with the tourists suffering throughout their time in Australia and New Zealand.

Wilf Gabbatt said in his official tour report following the interstate match: "This game was attended, and during same some free kicks were given for forward passes, the 10 yards radius rule was not operated, but the whole width of the field. Play-the-ball was crude and not in accordance with the rule, and similarly putting the ball into the scrum. At the conclusion of the game the referee, Mr McMahon [who refereed the two test matches in Sydney], approached Mr Popplewell and enquired if he was satisfied with the interpretation of the rules, and Mr Popplewell replied 'Yes'. I immediately strongly protested against this agreement, especially in view of the fact that Mr Popplewell and myself had not compared notes before expressing any opinion." He continued that in his view problems over interpretation of the rules continued in Australia and New Zealand.

Before the players left Sydney, they were given the opportunity to use a local sports arena to train. The newspaper reports of the tourists' periods of practice make somewhat strange reading. Already many reporters were implying that they looked much slower than their predecessors, and also appeared not to have the same ball skills. The players themselves must have had many a smile about what was being reported; particularly before even they had played a match in anger.

All too soon the early pleasantries were over, and the Lions were now faced with two out-of-town games prior to the first of the New South Wales matches, which would both be played in Sydney. The players no doubt welcomed the brief respite away from the pack of Sydney journalists, and were able to get down to the serious business of retaining the Ashes.

The Welsh players, with two Warrant Officers on the flight deck, 21 April. (DP)

The tour party on the Indomitable. (RFL/DJ)

Sightseeing in Aden on a welcome break from life on board. (RFL/DJ)

Ward, Hughes, Whitcombe, Owens, Bassett and Phillips
asleep on the train journey from Perth to Sydney. (DP)

23

Queuing up for food at Kalgoorlie camp for troops
while traveling from Perth to Sydney. (DP)

The Welsh Choir singing at Melbourne station on their way to Sydney. (DP)

# 4. Early days

The Australian rugby league authorities had now taken over from the Australian government in managing the travel arrangements. Even so problems became evident when the party had to split into two groups. Because of the tight playing schedule, the players who were not selected for a country game would stay at the tourists' base hotel, and then meet up later with their team-mates ready for the following fixture. To be fair to their hosts, there were always going to be problems, because the government had stringent travelling restrictions in place all across Australia, to cover the drastic fuel shortages brought on by the war. The government was left with no option but to build up sufficient fuel reserves, in order to assist the Australian economy to recover. The tourists became used to making their own arrangements as to how to get to various destinations.

They often found the trains so slow that a number of the more energetic players would run alongside for exercise. One of the tourists' jokes was that Fred Hughes, not noted for his sprinting prowess, could all too often outrun the train. While the Australian government had made the overtures in seeking a post-war tour, they clearly expected the managing committee of the Australian Rugby League to be competent enough to take control of the tour arrangements, and there must have been many occasions when the touring party became frustrated with that organisation.

After the tourists were visited by the troop of local reporters in Sydney, the players quickly learnt the basic lesson that one did not complain about Australian cordiality, because a wrong word always brought reports of the tourists being champion whingers. A small remark could be grossly inflated. Yet to be fair to their hosts, the tourists were now being treated as major stars, and the cream of Sydney society entertained the tourists.

After such a long journey, the tourists were in no hurry to get down to heavy match practice, and their measure of loosening-up, which included a number of the faster players wearing running shoes, did not go down too well with a number of the Australian reporters who were observing the practise sessions. Remarks in the press included such comments as, "many of the players appeared smaller than in previous years", apart from Frank Whitcombe and the other props. Frank found himself written off as a fat overweight player, who would need to lose a lot of weight to be mobile enough for international rugby. The goalkickers in the party also came in for their fair share of the criticism, and were regarded as not consistently accurate. The tourists' passing movements were considered too telegraphed, and certainly were not expected to open Australian defences. In short, the standards of the 1946 touring side from the media point of view fell far short of the standards set by previous Lions tourists.

As if this was not enough, the press corps was now commenting on the appearance of the tourists, and their observations were that they were lacking the tall guardsman appearance, which had been a noticeable feature of previous touring sides.

To really stress the negatives, the press used comments from former Australian test players, who were quick to emphasise that they had formerly played against tourist sides who were streets ahead of these modern day players. However, it should be observed that they were clearly just as critical of their own players, as well as the tourists. Obviously, memories lead to exaggeration, and improve former talents. As people age they are apt to embellish their prowess, and certainly these former Australian players followed that line.

Australia had not won a test series against England since 1920, and reading the comments of the former Kangaroos, it was clear that this would be due to an overall decline in playing standards, since these former players' playing days, and certainly not because the 1946 Australian players were any better than their predecessors.

The one tourist who had impressed the writers was Tommy McCue. They now rated him as probably the world's best scrum half, and they thought it was probable he would be a permanent thorn in the side of the Australians. Following the opening matches they gave faint praise to such as Ernest Ward, Willie Horne and Ike Owens. The latter had shown some of the flashes of his speed in the opening games of the tour, but any praise was countered by saying that they had been allowed to run by sub-standard defences.

Certainly, it was expected that New South Wales would not give them the same opportunity to exaggerate their skills, and more importantly the same space to operate in. The British forwards overall were regarded as yards slower than the New South Wales pack, which, it was suggested, would have a field day against them. Many of these comments were based on reports from out-of-town reporters, because the main Sydney sports writers did not feel the need to observe the tourists' two opening matches against country sides.

A player who impressed the Australians was Gus Risman, who was well known from his pre-war tour, and was clearly a captain who would lead by example. And Joe Egan, at hooker, was rated as one of the fastest strikers of a ball in the scrums they had ever seen. It was already clear that he would ensure the British side had a good percentage of possession in the forthcoming matches. The skill of Tommy McCue at half-back was thought likely to be complemented by the artistry of Willie Horne, although the latter did look somewhat frail for test rugby. This pair could perhaps develop into a strong partnership as they played together more on the tour.

Left: Doug Phillips and the *Australian Sun's* Bill Corbett at the Port Leeuwin Naval Barracks, Freemantle. (DP)

Below: Training at Sydney No. 2 ground – Joe Egan, Harry Murphy and Doug Phillips facing Frank Whitcombe. (DP)

Away from rugby, Ike Owens had a musical background, as his father was the conductor of the local church choir in the mining valley where he was born. His father at an early age had recruited him and his brother into the choir, added to which the Owens family were also involved with the Valley colliery brass band, with Owens senior being the solo trombonist. During the preceding long sea voyage, Ike had assembled the Welsh players into a male voice choir, which had helped to pass the time. They must have practised hard, because they were not only appreciated at receptions for the tourists, but figured regularly on an Australian radio programme.

The players also went to the cinema, theatre and dances, as well as the official receptions organised for them.

## Southern Districts

The tourists' opening match was against Southern Districts. They had to travel more than 260 miles by train to get there, and it took 8½ hours. The match was played at Junee which at that time was a railway town, and sheep and wheat farming centre. Junee is an Aboriginal word for 'speak to me'. Today the town has a population of just under 5,000. It is very proud that Laurie Daley, the Australian rugby league immortal was born there. In the 1940s a comedian called Bill Kerr was making a name for himself in Britain and, although from South Africa, always got a laugh by saying he came from a place called Wagga Wagga. The tourists must have smiled to themselves to find this unusually named place was just nearby. At the time there were big plans for Junee to be the hub of the railway system for New South Wales, with a huge engine shed and turntable in the process of being erected. Unfortunately, steam railways are not a major part of modern Australian transport, but the engine shed survives, and is the home of a popular railway museum.

Despite the small population, 6,135 attended the game, paying £649. It was the first time a touring team had played in Junee. This was an early indication of the large attendances which would be seen at future matches. The tourists faced opponents who gave them very few problems, and the Lions won easily, 36–4. This was a comfortable workout for the tourists, but as often happens in this type of warm-up match, a number of niggling injuries were picked up. Phillips and Nicholson were both injured, and some other injuries surfaced in the next few days, probably due to the long break from the game.

As with most of the country matches, the Lions' visit was a big occasion. George Thatcher, one of the Australian journalists, wrote that "The whole of Junee turned out this evening to welcome the English Rugby League team. All shops were closed at 4.45, three quarters of an hour earlier than usual. All accommodation in the town is booked out, as their train approached all the locomotives in the work sheds sounded their whistles, and every car sounded their horns. A sumptuous feast was held that evening for the Lions who ate six turkeys." Another report has the dinner including three pigs as well as turkeys. For players who had been used to army food or rations at home, it must have been difficult to keep to a good playing weight.

The party was in Junee for a couple of days, and then had a train journey of almost 10 hours to return to Sydney.

The journalists were now more positive about the team. W.F. Corbett said in the *Sydney Sun* that "Ernest Ward is a great centre and the combination of the whole side is a treat to watch". George Thatcher wrote in the *Telegraph* that "Owens's speed is an eye opener... Ernest Ward and Foster are also outstanding in a side which played exhilarating open football that will delight the Sydney crowds." There were also reports that three tourists were to sign for Australian clubs – these continued throughout the tour.

It was already becoming inevitable that a number of players would have to play consecutive matches later in the tour, due to the inexplicable whim of the selectors who decided to take an extra back in the squad, and bring only 11 forwards. There had been some concerns within the British camp that the tour would have two separate teams playing, one for test and representative games, and the other for the country matches.

Some of the press had not been very impressed with the tourists' overall play in the opening match. Apart from some of what they called tricky back flick passing, they considered that the side did not look good enough, or have sufficient skills to challenge the New South Wales state side in the forthcoming match.

Before they could play the state side, a match was arranged in the capital, Canberra, against a local team, Group 8, based in the Southern Tablelands. Australian Rugby League historian Sean Fagan outlined that "The NSW Rugby League divided the state into regions, within each region the area is divided into groups. The first grade clubs in Group 8 in 1946 were Canberra, Queanbeyan, Captains Flat, Goulburn, Yass and Crookwell. Of those towns, only Canberra is in the ACT, the rest are all in NSW." The Governor, the Duke of Gloucester was planning to attend, and it was the intention of the tour management that every member of the party would get a game under their belts.

The trip meant another six hour train journey. Despite the low level of the opposition, and its late inclusion in the tour schedule, it was to cause long term difficulties to the touring side's selection for future matches. The Lions' captain and vice-captain did not play. Ted Ward was nominated captain for the day.

The *Canberra Times* headline was "Group 8 plays stirring rugby against English team", and it was not a gentle workout for the tourists.

The tourists about to get on a bus in Sydney. (RFL/DJ)

Looking at a photograph album with William McKell, the Labor New South Wales Prime Minister on 16 May 1946. (DP)

Ted Ward, Doug Phillips, Gus Risman, Joey Jones and Ike Owens singing in *The Corn is Green* at the Minerva Theatre in Sydney. (DP)

Dai Jenkins pulling a pint in Sydney. (RFL/DJ)

Supporters at the first match in Junee. (DP)

Harry Murphy shaking hands with the Governor of Australia,
the Duke of Gloucester at Canberra. (DP)

The tourists inspecting the Speaker's chair at
Government House, Canberra. (DP)

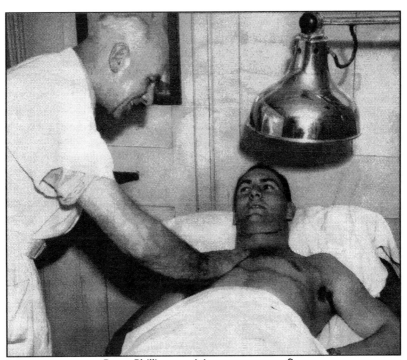

Doug Phillips receiving a massage after
getting a knock in the Canberra game. (DP)

The local players played as if their lives depended on it. Fortunately for the Lions, they did not have a recognised kicker, as the tourists were heavily penalised for play-the-ball infringements but, despite this, the referee, Allan Armstrong, praised the tourists saying they were real gentlemen on the field of play.

Everyone agreed that the game had been played in a very sporting manner despite some undue physical play by the home side. Unfortunately, the tourists – who had won 45–12, scoring 11 tries – sustained a number of injuries which ruled out more players for future matches. Harry Murphy had been having an outstanding match when he fell from a tackle, landed on his shoulder and dislocated it. Sadly, he was not able to play for the rest of the tour as it was discovered he had broken his collarbone. Harry was nicknamed Garth after a *Daily Mirror* cartoon character with a very muscular build, and would be badly missed. Joey Jones was thought to have sprained a finger but subsequently this would prove to require surgery. Bob Nicholson had difficulties breathing during the game, and was found to have pleurisy which ruled him out of the next 12 matches. To complete the tourists' misery, both Doug Phillips and Fred Hughes had also picked up injuries which also ruled them out of the New South Wales match. Fred's injury became exacerbated by arthritis. He was also a lifelong sufferer from gout, for which there was little treatment available at this time. The hard physical matches would not have helped his condition. Alfred Drewry reported that "...The tourists are left with only three reserve forwards before the really serious programme has begun."

The Australian journalist W.F. Corbett said that "England will need a thorough grooming on how to play the ball. If Group 8 had a kicker the score would have been tight... The English players not playing stated it was one of the cleanest matches they had seen."

Following this game the tourists met and decided that they would start wearing body padding, which was the general practice of the Australian players. Certainly with the hardness of the grounds it was a wise precaution. Body padding in Britain had up until now not been in general use, and was not usually considered necessary.

The tourists travelled back on the train overnight from Canberra following the match, arriving in Sydney at 5.25am. Doug Phillips recalled that he could not sleep on the train because of the pain from his injury.

## New South Wales

The tourists' team selection for the first of the state games was in doubt almost to the moment of kick-off, as the players were still suffering after-effects of the Canberra game. Phillips, who had extensive physiotherapy, had a sleepless night, and had to withdraw, but fortunately Martin Ryan passed a late fitness test.

The tourists had visited the Sydney Cricket Ground (SCG) soon after their arrival in Sydney to see New South Wales beat Queensland 24–6 before a crowd of 27,866. To mark the occasion Gus Risman had been given the honour of kicking off the game.

The crowd build-up for the match against New South Wales began early, with a large queue forming at the gates even before dawn broke. Despite the prevailing transport restrictions, the public was clearly not going to be deterred from attending the biggest game since the war. A massive 51,364 spectators attended this match and they were supplemented by the membership of the New South Wales cricket club, which numbered 10,000 all of whom had the rights to watch all other major sporting events besides cricket matches at the SCG. The receipts were £6,012, which was only surpassed by the massive crowd for the first test.

The attendance gave some indication of the huge numbers who would attend the forthcoming test matches. Many spectators had been willing to queue all night. Local reporters were claiming that if similar numbers were to be let into the ground for the test matches, then spectator safety could be at risk.

When the sides ran out onto the famous ground, the roar was deafening and, as was to be expected, hostile to the tourists.

In the first half it became increasingly obvious that the tourists were under orders to play a defensive game, and to get the feel of playing under Australian conditions. What attacking play that took place in the first half was Australian-inspired, but after much pressure the home side had only one try to show for their efforts. If the tourists had not still been showing some early rustiness they could quite easily have scored twice. Trevor Foster, of all people, managed to drop the ball with the line wide open before him. Then the ever-reliable Gus Risman threw a wild pass with players in support, and once again the try line open, after he had been put through by Owens from a scrum. The score at half-time was only 7–0 to the state side, although a highly charged burst of play from the home side in the first 10 minutes of the second half almost led to them taking an unassailable lead.

First, Pat Devery, the New South Wales half-back, broke through but at the last moment Owens managed to catch him, and threw him into touch with the British line completely open. But there was no stopping Lionel Cooper who scored a fine diving try, a movement he would repeat so many times in future years for Huddersfield. The try, fortunately for the Lions, was not converted. So despite the early non-stop pressure on the British defence, the home side were only 10–0 ahead. This helped give the tourists more confidence.

This sudden activity, and the constant pressure of the Australians made the tourists realise they must step up their game. McCue, ever

Publicity photo with the players wearing 'Stamina' trousers
which they were given free. (DP)

Watching the first match against New South Wales: Seated: Ernest Ward, Ted
Ward, Bryn Knowelden, Frank Whitcombe, Wilf Gabbatt, Walter Popplewell,
Tommy McCue and Ken Gee; on ground: Jack Kitching, Fred Hughes,
Doug Phillips, Willie Horne and Willie Davies. (DP)

the master craftsman, started to take control behind the scrums and he gave Owens an easy try with the New South Wales defence caught out of position. Risman comfortably converted.

The Australian defence began to panic at the pressure now being placed upon them, and gave away two silly penalties in front of their own posts. Risman kicked both, making the score 10–9 to New South Wales. The game now began to become heated and Trevor Foster was involved in a midfield melee with an Australian forward. This was followed by Frank Whitcombe being given a severe reprimand for some illegal work in the scrums. Then both hookers fell foul of the referee's wrath, were told off, and looked suitably chastened.

Ryan, the tourists' full-back gathered a high kick near his line, and set off on a length-of-the-field run. The reporters said that he was assisted by some careful shepherding from his teammates. He was stopped in front of the home posts, but the damage had been done and the tourists quickly moved the ball away from the centre of the Australian defence. A long pass went out to Eric Batten on the wing, and he scored a relatively easy try – his markers being out of position.

The crowd had kept up a deafening crescendo, but was now suddenly silent. Then the spectators' emotions were severely tested by Risman's conversion. Many were sure that the ball had not gone between the posts, but the kick was allowed and gave the Lions a 14–10 lead. Alfred Drewry wrote that "Risman is quite sure his shot at goal passed outside, but flags went up and England were credited with two points they did not earn."

The fans' feelings were further incensed after the restart, when the kick-off was caught just in front of the British posts. The resultant Australian charge led to a rather frustrated punch-up. Alas for the home side, the resultant melee only brought the final whistle a little closer, and while there remained time for a couple of attacks on the British defence, they were hardly coordinated following rushed passes. A full scale New South Wales assault on the British defensive line thus failed to emerge.

Trevor Foster recalls the match as the first time he played against Arthur Clues: "Every time I received the ball I was knocked for six by Arthur." They faced each other many times when Clues joined Leeds in 1947, and despite their different temperaments became close friends.

Doug Phillips reflected in his diary that the win "...was dubious. The boys didn't play well at all, especially first half."

The Lions side was:

Martin Ryan, Eric Batten, Ernest Ward, Gus Risman ( c ), Albert Johnson, Willie Horne, Tommy McCue, Ken Gee, Joe Egan, Frank Whitcombe, Les White, Trevor Foster, Ike Owens.

## Ike Owens comes to prominence

The next match was the following day, Sunday 2 June, against a South Coast team at Wollongong. The tourists, besides the indignity of losing 15–12 in a closely fought game – and fought is probably the correct term – were now faced with major injury problems. Trevor Foster suffered what appeared at first to be an innocuous knee injury, but this led to major problems for him for much of the tour. Trevor recalled in his biography: "I felt really good that day, extremely fit and ready to take on the world. I was looking forward to playing in the first test match... It was a rather innocuous tackle from the side, one of their forwards took me by surprise. I fell at an awkward angle and my left knee buckled under my weight as I hit the ground. I knew immediately that there was some serious damage. I could not straighten the leg and the knee swelled up like a balloon within a few seconds. For the first time in my career I had to be helped off." Trevor did not play again until 13 July.

Due to the overzealous play of their opponents and a rather lenient referee, the number of players picking up injuries was rapidly reaching epidemic proportions. Near the end of this match the tourists had almost as many injured players on the field as fit ones, and the managers took the decision that towards the end of the second half it would be better playing with a reduced number of players, rather than players aggravating the knocks they had already received.

The Lions had to play New South Wales again in the next match the following Saturday, who were now resolved to prove that the previous result would be well and truly overturned. So there would be little or no respite before the first test which was due to be played on Monday 17 June.

The harder grounds, which suited the faster players such as Ike Owens, were also having an adverse effect on many of the tourists. This was showing in the form of scrapes and abrasions. In those days they took longer to heal and all too often became infected. The use of penicillin was extremely limited at this time, and most infections were treated with sulphonamides which were not as effective. In fact, many of the players had to continue playing when it was clear that they were only half fit. There was no way that replacements could be sent from Britain.

The more the difficulties and hardships of the 1946 tourists become clear, their firm resolve to override the hardships they endured without a word of complaint becomes more admirable. The injured players did their utmost to recover and get back in the side as quickly as possible so that they could share the playing load with their colleagues.

The one bright spot from the South Coast match was the form of Ike Owens. He had a superb game, and many of the Australian press were now beginning to ask where he had come from, and what his pedigree was. Such was his stature and form in this match that many of the press regarded the match as Owens versus the South Coast. When he was in possession of the ball the other side had found it almost impossible to tackle him, and the Australian newsmen reckoned he could be a potential match winner for the tourists if given too much room and space to dominate.

Despite their travelling and playing commitments, the tourists also found time for leisure activities. Wilf Gabbatt commented in his tour report: "On June 3 and 4, at the invitation of the Australian Government, we visited Jenolan Caves. This was a welcome diversion and thoroughly enjoyed by all... On June 6 I called the attention of Mt Popplewell to what, in my opinion, to the effect that too much attention was being given to social activities and insufficient time to the requirements of the tour, adding that the players had not produced the form which gained them selection in the touring side. Subsequently a curfew was instituted, but as afar as I could perceive, was not enforced even the first night it was supposed to be in operation." Wilf Gabbatt was the business manager, with Walter Popplewell having responsibility for the playing side. Reading between the lines of his report, maybe Gabbatt was frustrated at times with his lack of influence over the players.

**New South Wales - again**

Another massive crowd gathered at the Sydney Cricket Ground ready to see the state side get their revenge. This was also the final opportunity for the New South Wales players to press for a place in the test team. Once again queues outside the ground started at dawn Unfortunately, their wishes were not going to be met, and they were about to see one of the most devastating displays of rugby by an individual opponent, which would be talked about for many a day. The Australian press, which had been full of comments and criticism about the tourists' lack of speed, were about to eat their words. Before the kick off, the areas around the ground were packed with spectators. They were in fine voice as they prepared to urge their heroes on.

The home side were in trouble from as early as the third minute when Owens gathered a relieving kick from the Australians, and immediately threw the defence into panic when he raced forward directly at the New South Wales tacklers, drawing the home defence with him out to the left flank and then calmly punted the ball across the field to where Frank Whitcombe was standing completely unmarked with the home line open. Unfortunately for the Lions, the big forward was unable to ground the ball after it bounced awkwardly over the home try line.

Joe Egan and Doug Phillips in action against New South Wales
(second match). (DP)

Doug Phillips and Eric Batten try their strength at a farm in Orange,
New South Wales. (DP)

If the Australians thought they could sit back and relax now that danger had been averted, they were wrong. Once again the visitors surged forward and attacked directly in front of the posts. Only a blatant obstruction prevented a try from being scored. From the resultant penalty, Gus Risman had little trouble in getting the scoreboard moving, and shortly afterwards was able to kick another penalty following a further obstruction as the tourists attacked the New South Wales line.

However, the home side was not going to give the tourists the freedom of the park. There followed what was described by the press as a torrid period of play as the forwards of both sides clashed, and attempted to impose their control often, it must be said, unfairly.

During this period of play the referee was extremely busy. Alfred Drewry wrote that "There were many things that went on in the gruelling forward battle that would not have been tolerated by English referees." Joe Egan, along with his opposing hooker was cautioned, and Ken Gee was laid out, which action caused the home supporters to trumpet with glee. Les White and Whitcombe were the next players to face the referee's wrath, and only some very solid defence by the visitors kept the home side out. Their constant pressure, with the assistance of some refereeing that the tourists felt favoured the home side, just had to prevail. A kickable penalty was missed by the home side, but a second one almost immediately afterwards found its mark. The crowd seemed sure that at last the tourists would be beaten.

Immediately New South Wales were back on the attack, but only to find Owens intercepting a pass on his own line. He set off on a jinking run at top speed. Several of the Australians were in a position to tackle him but failed to catch him thanks to his pace, and such was their panic that they failed to see the hard-running Kitching coming up in support. Once Owens had all the Australian defenders' attention – those who had managed to get back in defence – and were in a position to stop him from scoring, he casually threw the ball to the unmarked Kitching who ran in to score the try. Risman had a very comfortable kick to convert, placing the tourists 9–2 ahead.

Almost immediately, the Lions were back on the attack following the resumption of play, and once again it was Owens leading the Australians in another bewildering dance. A scrum in front of the tourists' line led to the ball coming into Owens hands, leaving the Australians to guess whether he would pass or run with it. He chose the latter option, and left the New South Wales side in total confusion. There was one point where it appeared as if the whole Australian side was attempting to stop him.

The player who benefited this time from the loose-forward's dazzling play was Bassett, out on the wing. He easily gathered Owens's crossfield punt, and scored near the posts. Risman converted.

Once again the tourists broke away from their own 25-yard area, but this time their passing, which had been so brilliant in its build up, became over-elaborate, resulting in a dropped pass, and what should have been another scoring opportunity was allowed to slip. At half time the visitors had a 14–2 lead. The home supporters were barely able to raise a cheer for their side as they went to the dressing rooms. The press described New South Wales's first half play as being let down by weak positional play, while their general speed was second rate, and their tackling at times absolutely shocking.

The second half began very much as the first half finished with Owens completely fooling the home side's defence. Such was his elusiveness that it made the Australian tackling once more appear woeful. The Australians were already describing him as the best British touring loose-forward they had ever seen. The New South Wales players at this point must have wondered why he had chosen this match to make fools of them, as their attempts to get in the test selectors' good books were now looking a complete shambles.

Fortunately for the home side, the tourists were regularly falling foul of the referee over feeding the scrum. A steady stream of penalties started to give New South Wales a gradual positional advantage. This was further assisted by the referee now giving penalties for illegal tackles by the tourists. Unfortunately for the Australian supporters, the New South Wales kicker was having an off day, and he failed to convert any of the penalties, despite a number of them being in very kickable positions.

But the tourists were not finished, and this time Willie Davies showed the spectators that Owens was not the only Welshman who could throw dummies. He opened up the New South Wales defence and Joe Egan was presented with a very easy try, which once again Risman converted. But at least the home side would not finish without a try, and Lionel Cooper notched an unconverted try in the corner.

Just before the final whistle an Australian forward at last managed to stop Owens, but unfortunately for this player, the tackle was not within the rules of the game. Once again Risman stepped up to take the penalty, and to complete the scoring at 21–7.

Shortly afterwards, the referee's whistle brought an end to the home side's misery. There was a stunned silence from the 47,085 crowd. They were now aware that Australia would have to improve dramatically in all aspects of the game to produce the kind of play that was necessary for them to win the Ashes.

The Australian press praised the tourists' play, indicating that their tactics were far in advance of those of the home side. They were impressed by Gus Risman, saying that he had been a towering figure at the back of the defence, playing with cool resolution, and always finding the open spaces with his kicks. The Lions' pack was complemented on their tight control of play, and the only weakness they could find was a tendency to break the rules of the scrum.

Of course Owens came in for special praise, and following on from his display the week before, was rated as one of the best loose-forwards ever seen by the Australians. They described him as a match-winner, particularly the way he took play out wide from the scrums, looking for and creating openings. The supreme accolade for Owens was being described as a "player-and-a-half", and the openings he created for his team mates were described just as good as 10 extra points to the tourists. One headline read "Owens slaughters the Blues" and all the reporters believed that if Australia could not find an effective method of keeping him under control they could say goodbye to the Ashes.

Following the New South Wales match, the tourists had a comfortable match against Western Districts, winning 33–2. The team had a seven hour train journey to Orange. There was a reception for them in the evening, but Doug Phillips recalled that "The speeches were terrible." After the match the team returned overnight to Sydney, this time with sleeping cars. The crowd included a group of RAF servicemen who had travelled 120 miles to watch the Lions in action.

Unfortunately, this was the start of another spurt of injuries, and Trevor Foster, who appeared to be running into form, picked up what at first appeared to be an innocuous knee injury on the same knee as previously, and this injury would affect him for the rest of the Australian part of the tour. Several times on the tour both Trevor and the coaches thought he had recovered, but only to discover after a short run it was just as bad as before. Even worse was losing Joe Jones with an injury and left only Martin Ryan as a specialist full-back. Alfred Drewry commented on the shortage of fit forwards: "At the moment [Popplewell] has only seven fit forwards to call upon. The strain has been severe on men like White, Whitcombe and Owens, who have played in five matches out of six."

Two days before the first test the tourists lost to Newcastle 18–13. This defeat was caused by attempting to play a match so near to the test and trying where possible to rest players who would be involved in that match. The simple truth was that the majority of players who were rested were those who were already injured. The final straw was losing Martin Ryan through injury, for which he had to have an operation. This meant a possible major reshuffle in the test side selection. There were very few options left for the British selectors and they hoped that no one else developed any type of injury or illness before the big day.

After the Newcastle game, Ryan had severe discomfort in his groin, but hoped that with a night's rest he would be able to play in the test. The day before the match he went to catch a high ball, fell in pain,

43

and was rushed to hospital, where a hernia was diagnosed, which required emergency treatment. He listened to the match commentary on the radio in his hospital bed, surrounded by nurses having their photographs taken for the newspapers.

Up to now all the matches had been well attended, and the most serious concern was the number of injuries sustained by spectators falling from stand roofs. There were just not enough stewards or police to control the large crowds which had thronged into the grounds, with 8,318 at Orange, and 17,134 at Newcastle.

The general belief at this time, the view of the Australian government and the rugby league authorities, was that travel restrictions would ensure that ground capacities would not be breached. Clearly they were wrong. They expected few problems in controlling the test crowds because they expected the grounds would be adequate to hold all the supporters who wished to attend. They were remarkably complacent.

Another factor which appeared to be ignored was the number of members who would attend these games. The test matches took place at Australian cricket grounds, and there appeared to be an illogical thought that the cricket followers would not be interested in rugby league. But there was huge interest among Australians in sport, and only their own ruling bodies seem reluctant to accept this.

The matches prior to the opening test should have given the authorities fair warning that extra reserves of stewards and police would be needed, and extra safety precautions should be taken. One cartoon in a Sydney newspaper amusingly assessed the situation by showing a gatekeeper saying to his mate that although the crowd had been fine, a number would not be coming out, because they had been buried in the ground.

The management was also made somewhat more complacent by the weather forecast prior to the first and second tests, which indicated an unseasonal spell of cold and rainy weather. This led to scenes which are hard to believe today. Neither Sydney nor Brisbane could ever have experienced such huge crowds.

It is debatable whether the Brisbane test should ever have been allowed to proceed, but then who would be brave enough to make the decision to stop the match so that the crowd could be reduced? If the matches had been called off the spectators could have rioted.

Such was the interest the test series was arousing that many of the tourists were rapidly becoming public icons. Trevor Foster in an interview with the *Yorkshire Evening Post* mentioned this. Players such as Gus Risman and Ike Owens could hardly venture out without being mobbed, and the tourists had star status with the press hanging on to their every word. Never before can a touring side have reached such heights, and it is also only fair to add that the Australian public

44

appreciated them all the more following six years of war.

The Australian newspaper article below shows what the tour meant to the public. Of course, by football the article means rugby league.

## The English visit

"It may be true that Australians are disposed to go a little too far in their love of sport, to the neglect of other matters of import, the charge will not be permitted to lie as regards the intra-Empire contests which have grown up with the cricket and football tests, and certainly not in respect of the present football tour...

Perhaps no truer index of the British character could be cited than that, so soon after the guns had ceased roaring and whilst Britain is grappling with grave economic problems, this football team should be sent on a tour of Australia. Sticklers for the appropriateness of 'time and place' may shake a disapproving head and declare that this is something that could wait, yet is not the fact of the tour being undertaken the best notice that could be served, on the rest of the world, that Britain looks upon her post-war difficulties as transitory and has replaced the wartime slogan of 'business as usual' with a peace-time equivalent in 'sport as usual?'. It must be remembered, also, that football is the greatest safety valve of the British masses...

It may be questioned by the football fan whether this is one of the greatest touring teams ... ever [from] England. It would be surprising if it were... Nor does it matter one whit. If they lost every match it would be no disgrace to them, nor would it lessen the cordiality of our reception. On the football field, from the school game to the test match, there are heated moments, but there is also a code which decrees that these should not be magnified but forgiven in the convivial intermingling off the field. This is puzzling to outside nations. The recent Newcastle game between the Englishmen and the Northern coalfields would have sent the late Dr Goebbels into ecstasies, but he would have later been bewildered to note the warmth of the reception accorded the visitors wherever they journeyed. That is the great virtue of competitive sport as played in British communities...

There is a fundamental difference between intra-Empire and international sport. At the pre-war Olympic Games some European nations – to none did this apply more than the Germans – took the competitions so seriously that defeat was regarded as a national disgrace and feeling ran so high that the time appeared to be approaching when each Olympic team would have to be accompanied by a protective armed force. As in sport so it is with other aspects of Empire relations. Like all families the British family of nations is not always in complete harmony, but no divergence of view is ever likely to lead to permanent estrangement...

Apart from the national aspect, the visit of the Englishmen has an

45

importance from the sporting and historical side. The exhibition of the code given by players of the calibre of those who opposed our representatives yesterday is bound to have a beneficial influence on the local game, for experience will have been gained and points picked up by the local side. Historically the England versus Australian matches in 1946 will go down as noteworthy events in our sporting record, and remembered in years to come...

In later years when another English team plays in Australia it will be something to look back on... the first English tour after the war, when the ... men on both sides who had just come back from a more serious game on distant fields. As for the Englishmen, they may have learned little from us to improve their football, but we trust they will have found here, a feeling towards them and the land from which they come, as warm as any that could be offered by kinsmen."

Two match programmes (Courtesy Mike Inman)

# 5. The first test

As the first test match approached, the interest began to grow, and the Australian newspapers increased their coverage of rugby league. The tourists must have felt like goldfish with all the media interest in them. They must have been amazed when they compared it with the low key coverage which the sport often had at home.

Unfortunately for the Lions, they had struck a period when every match appeared to bring another major injury mishap to the team. What appeared at first to be minor problems later grew into major difficulties. The crisis now was the loss of both full-backs to injury. Indeed before the first test was played, it was clear that neither player would take any further part in the test matches, and both would only play a limited role in the rest of the tour.

Martin Ryan had the worst luck in that he was injured on the day before the test. Added to the loss of Foster, the extra demands of the tour matches meant some of the other forwards were suffering various strains, which they had been unable to rest, and playing regularly aggravated these injuries.

Another handicap was the average age of the players – injuries which are shrugged off more easily by young players, tend to become long-term in older players. With a party of only 26 players, one absentee meant that at least one other player had to play two matches in a week. Now the tourists had three players permanently out of action. The situation had not been helped by the players being called on to play two of the hardest non-test matches would play throughout the tour. These were against the New South Wales state side, who would supply many of the full Australian team. The other matches were against regional sides with players who often thought they should have been selected for the state, and had a point to prove. It was unfortunate that the tour fixtures did not include many club sides, which would have been easier games before the first test.

This was not commented on much by the Lions, but surprisingly by a number of Australian supporters in letters to the Sydney newspapers. Certainly a major factor in the itinerary was that due to the war many of the major club sides were not particularly strong.

The inclement weather gave the Australians their first touch of winter. But despite the rain and cold, the crowds were quite happy to queue and wait all night outside the ground. It was a public holiday for the King's birthday. The growing numbers made it apparent at dawn that the "house full" notices would very soon be on display. From first light, every arriving tram car and bus from Sydney was packed with supporters eager to see the match. Every horse and cart which was available was put to good use, with motor cars clearly ignoring petrol shortages. Thousands made their way to the famous ground. At 10.30am, the decision was taken by the police to close the gates, much to the crowd's disgust. Further chaos arose when it was realised that the main entrance for members was being kept open. Resentment arose because the members' enclosure was not full, and the crowds charged forward in an attempt to gain access there. Later a number of spectators – a very small number – came out of the ground demanding their money back, because they said it was impossible to see the playing area and there were instances of people throwing their lunch wrappings into the air, supposedly to show their disgust at having a poor view of the pitch.

No one could ever complain about this test match having no atmosphere and, to keep matters on the boil long before play was due to begin, what infamously became known as the 'Battle of Sydney Hill' broke out. There were two participating groups, one being the season-ticket membership, from the Sydney cricket club, and the other being made up of rugby league supporters. The conflict consisted of people laying their hands on every scrap of rubbish they could find and then throwing it at the others. The press described these incidents as like being in a rubbish blizzard. One litter storm lasted over half an hour.

Fortunately, no one was seriously injured and probably these incidents helped to defuse any further bad feeling which could have arisen from battling to get into the ground, combined with the long wait for the match to begin. There is no doubt that the cricket members carried a lot of influence, and they were the main force behind the police decision to close the ground so early. This was because they did not want their view from the cricket pavilions blocked by the standing spectators who had gained entrance on the day.

The cheekiest gatecrasher of all was a gentleman, who entered the hotel where the tourists were staying and began talking in a broad Yorkshire accent. He soon got into conversation with Frank Whitcombe, and spoke of having watched him at Broughton Rangers before he transferred to Bradford. While Frank went to fetch his kit ready to go to the match, his new-found friend offered to look after Frank's blazer until he came back to the reception area. Needless to say, when Frank returned his so-called friend had disappeared with his blazer. The story had a happy ending for both parties, as the stranger got into the ground and Frank got his blazer back.

The teams lined up as follows:
*Australia:* Dave Parkinson, Edgar Newham, Joe Jorgenson ( c ), Ron Bailey, Lionel Cooper, Pat Devery, John Grice, Frank Farrell, George Watt, Roy Westaway, Arthur Clues, Reg Kay, Noel Mulligan.
*Great Britain:* Gus Risman ( c ), Eric Batten, Ernest Ward, Jack Kitching, Albert Johnson, Willie Horne, Tommy McCue, Ken Gee, Joe Egan, Frank Whitcombe, Doug Phillips, Les White, Ike Owens.
*Referee:* T. McMahon

Except for Gus Risman and Tommy McCue, all the players were making their debuts in official test matches for their respective sides. However, all the Great Britain players had represented England or Wales in the European Championship, and many of the players had played in wartime international matches.

Four of the Australian team went on to have successful careers in British rugby league. Arthur Clues, who played for Leeds, became a great favourite there and gave them many years outstanding service. Lionel Cooper, a truly outstanding winger became a Huddersfield legend and was almost unstoppable near the try line. Pat Devery also joined Huddersfield in 1947, and scored over 1,000 points in England. George Watt signed for Hull in 1947, and played 90 games in four seasons, and briefly played for Rochdale before returning to Australia.

All these players were allowed to move as the international transfer ban between Australia and Great Britain had not been renewed. Australian rugby league historians Alan Whiticker and Ian Collis wryly commented that: "With the lifting of the international poaching bans, the wealthy English clubs plundered the best players Australia had to offer." In August 1947 the ban was reinstated.

Ike Owens was playing for Leeds at this time, and would soon have Clues as a team mate. In later years he played with Cooper and Devery in an outstanding Huddersfield team who, for a time in the late 1940s and early 1950s, were almost unbeatable.

Harry Bath, who missed the test series through injury, was another player to have great success in England. Another player in contention for an Australian test place was Ray Lindwall, who subsequently decided to concentrate on cricket, where he became one of the world's leading fast bowlers.

**The Lions**

The Lions team was different from that predicted in the newspapers and the official programme because Martin Ryan was, of course, missing with his late injury. He returned to Australia with the 1950 Lions and became generally recognised as one of the finest attacking full-backs in rugby league. Prior to the Second World War, most full-backs were noted for having long kicking duels against their opposite number and played a very defensive role. Ryan was one of the first full-backs to run directly at the opposition after catching the ball, and to play a supporting role to the threequarters when his side was attacking their opponents' line.

Gus Risman took over the full-back role, and Bradford's Jack Kitching was drafted into the threequarters, a move which was to have a dramatic effect on events during the match. The positional changes would certainly affect Risman who was fast approaching an age when many players would be thinking of retiring from professional rugby league. Observers felt that he had slowed up considerably, certainly compared to his previous appearances in Australia before the war. Many of the players who were contemporaries of Risman, describe him as the most complete rugby player they ever played alongside but sadly, age is no respecter of earlier capabilities.

The stadium erupted when the players appeared on the field and the Sydney Oval was certainly no place to be for the faint-hearted. All the cheers, as to be expected, were reserved for the home side, and the visitors were then met by a storm of booing and abuse. If a crowd could lift its side, then the Australians must have felt ultra confident. Joe Jorgenson, the home skipper, won the toss, and then followed the quietest part of the afternoon, while the National Anthem was played. The massive crowd was then given the opportunity to gather its vocal strength before kick-off. There followed another huge roar as Tommy McCue started the game with a deep kick into the Australian half of the field, but it was as if the Australian side had succumbed to an attack of nerves after encountering the atmosphere in the ground. The Lions should have scored in the opening minutes, as the Australians committed a silly infringement in the first scrum of the match. Very uncharacteristically, Risman missed the penalty from only 10 yards in front of the posts.

The Lions maintained this early pressure and opened the scoring after only two minutes, with Willie Horne crossing the line after John Grice fumbled. His speed and dexterity then allowed him to place the ball closer to the posts for a very kickable conversion. Unfortunately, this was one of those rare occasions when Risman had failed to put his kicking boots on, and once again he missed. It was all the more surprising following his reliable kicking in the matches building up to the test. Certainly, he was not the type of character to be swayed by a large crowd, and Gus Risman over the years was known throughout rugby league as one of the game's most reliable goalkickers. Yet he had one of those days when everything appeared to go wrong.

The Australians very soon recovered their composure, and were not long in reducing the deficit. Ken Gee and his opposite number Frank 'Bumper' Farrell, had a strong verbal exchange, which was followed by Gee slapping Farrell's face. The resultant penalty was well taken by Jorgenson from 35 yards out and so, after only six minutes play, and because of Risman's misses, the score was now 3–2 to the tourists. But the Lions were then to enjoy a long period of domination, with most of the play taking place in the Australian half of the field. The Australians were put under such pressure that they gave penalties away. Some of these were from a very kickable range but, sadly Risman just could not get on target. On a couple of occasions the visitors were almost through the last line of the Australian defence, but each time some very fine last-ditch tackles saved the day. Having ridden out this onslaught, it was now the home side's turn to go on to the offensive, and scrum-half John Grice was caught just before he crossed the visitors' line.

It was now the tourists' turn to withstand sustained pressure. After a number of successive tackles had kept the Australians out, Owens at last gave the tourists' defence some much needed relief. He ran with the ball from his own line and left a number of Australian would-be tacklers grasping at thin air. He was finally stopped on the halfway line by a number of Australian defenders. This ploy was enough for the Lions to finally ease the Australian attacking storm. Then some darting speedy runs from the England backs put the Australian defence under pressure once more.

The home side turned the tables and after a breakaway run, which was followed by a downfield kick by the Australians, Risman had the misfortune to knock on in his own 25-yard area. Unfortunately for the Australians, the Lions won the resultant scrum against the head. Once again pressure was relieved by Owens who went on one of his weaving runs. Even better this time he was able to set up a springboard for Britain to attack. The Australians were unsure how to deal with the loose-forward and, after he had drawn the Australian defence, he put out a long pass to Batten, who appeared to have a clear run for the line. It looked a certain try, but after a Herculean effort by Cooper and Newham, he was stopped just inches short of scoring. However, Cooper was knocked senseless in this superb try-saving effort and needed treatment from the trainer to recover.

The most serious incident in the match took place in the 27th minute. Jack Kitching, the Lions' centre, and the Australian captain Jorgenson were the two players involved. After being tackled by the Australian, Kitching received his marching orders for allegedly pushing the Australian skipper's head into the ground, which the referee deemed to be striking his opponent. But this was just a prelude to the most controversial incident that rugby league had ever witnessed, and for Australians was almost as notorious as the 1932–33 'Bodyline' cricket controversy.

Certainly, if the British press of the time had covered rugby league more widely the British public would have been more aware that diplomatic relations between Australia and Britain were about to come under threat. This was because on Kitching's return to the dressing room, he claimed that he had only retaliated because he had been bitten on his chest, and he had the marks to prove it. Never had the game seen such divisions, but all that was for after the match. The immediate problem was that the Lions side had nearly quarter of an hour of the first half to play with a man short, and of course they would have to prepare for the second half with only 12 men.

The Lions had to alter their team line-up. Owens moved to play at centre, and the tourists had to grit its teeth, perhaps an unfortunate metaphor in the circumstances, and play on with the pack now a man short. They responded to this adversity magnificently and only three minutes after the dismissal, Frank Whitcombe, the giant man-mountain prop, forced his way over the try line despite the attention of three Australian defenders. This try was the result of a quick passing movement instigated by the half-backs following which Ernest Ward made a darting run, kicking forward before getting the ball out to Johnson

Jack Kitching leaving the field after being sent off. (RFL/DJ)

who put Whitcombe in near the corner. Once again Risman failed to convert. Just before half-time, Batten broke clear on his own touchline, and caused the spectators to gasp when he performed his well-known party piece and jumped over a defender, going for the open tryline. Once again, the alert Lionel Cooper was alive to the danger, and managed to stop Batten just short of the line. There was no further change to the score leading up to half-time, and the referee's whistle to end play must have been a very welcome sound to the British players.

**The second half**

For the second half, the Lions once again changed a number of positions in their line-up, and Owens now moved to play his third position of the match, this time at prop forward. Eric Batten moved into the centre, and White moved out to the wing. Reports indicate that these changes did little to improve the Lions' play. They now appeared to be disjointed, and had difficulty in setting up any form of passing movement. It was at this stage of the game, and with the Australians starting to exert some supremacy, that the Lions were fortunate that their hooker, Joe Egan, was able to win the ball against the head on a number of occasions. This enabled the Lions to maintain possession, especially when defending near their own line. Egan was to have an outstanding tour and was never in the position of being outplayed by an Australian hooker.

Behind the scrum was one of the best half-back combinations

52

Britain has ever had, and which was to cause chaos and dismay to the opposing Australian defences. Horne and McCue, with Owens at loose-forward, could almost mind-read each other, and throw the opposing defenders subtle dummies so that they were continually sent the wrong way. Despite the imbalance within the tourists' line-up, the early part of the second half saw no further score, despite both the tourists and the home side being awarded penalties – Risman and Jorgensen both missed.

The Australians at last started making the pressure of an extra man begin to tell and, after 11 minutes of the second half, Ron Bailey was able to break through in a strong, purposeful Australian attack, and completely wrong-foot Risman. He was fully expecting Bailey to pass, and he was able to run through to score an easy try, with the Lions' line completely broken. Fortunately for the tourists, Australia once more were unable to convert, but the tourists' lead had now been cut to only one point. They must certainly have breathed a sigh of relief when Risman converted a penalty under the Australians' posts when Farrell was caught offside. This made the score 8–5 to the Lions.

In the build-up in play prior to the penalty, McCue had received a very heavy tackle, which completely knocked him out. Though he soon recovered consciousness, he had to go off the field for a short while in order to fully recover, and so the tourists were down to 11 players on the field. Clever play between Horne and Owens led to the Lions easing the pressure, but sadly there was no one able to back up Owens, which is hardly surprising in the circumstances. It was becoming clear that if the Lions were to score a try it would have to be an individual attempt.

The home crowd was now fully behind their team, and with every prospect of its heroes achieving an opening victory in the test series, it was now giving full vocal encouragement. The noise was absolutely deafening. The tackling was now torrid to say the least, and no quarter was being given or asked. The next tourist to need treatment was Johnson who, while chasing a loose ball, felt the full force of a high Clues tackle. The Warrington winger had already faced some very ferocious tackling, and had become a target for the Australians. While there was legitimate tackling, some of it seemed questionable. The pressure was now being put once more onto the Lions, and even more so when Australia equalised after 25 minutes of the second half. This time it was Cooper breaking away on a clear 60 yard run, and then comfortably deceiving Risman to score out wide. But once more, like most of the goalkicks in this game, the home side missed the conversion. So the score remained at 8–8. This led to a nail biting finish, and the home crowd was now fully behind their national idols. The roar of excitement when Cooper had scored was said to have been heard around the whole of Sydney. But both sides were determined to score, and on several occasions it looked as if the defences had been pierced, yet more of the scoring opportunities were now falling to Australia.

The crowd's roar suddenly fell silent, when McCue broke away from the scrum with White and Owens backing up. Owens then took the ball on and comfortably slipped past two opponents, then headed at full speed towards the Australian line. The roar that went up from the crowd was as much relief as praise – the Australian defenders eventually managed to force Owens into touch just short of the line. Risman then attempted to score from a penalty awarded 10 yards inside the Australian half, but his kick fell well short of its destination. To be fair, even if his kicking had been up to its normal form, it would have needed an exceptional kick to have reached the target.

In the end, both players and crowd were able to relax when Jorgenson kicked into touch just as the referee blew his whistle for the end of play. Credit must go to the tourists for holding the home side to a draw after playing the match a man short for 50 minutes of the game. The result meant they were in a powerful position because they needed just one win in the final two tests to retain the Ashes.

**Injured players**

The Lions also hoped that before the next test in Brisbane a number of their injured players would be fit to return, and especially that the problem position of full-back could be successfully resolved. Even if the players who were not in contention for the test team due to injury recovered, they would allow players to have a break from the continuous grind of playing matches close together. The major problem lay in the forwards. Selection options were limited and they were the players who had to do the non-stop heavy tackling. While the return of players such as Trevor Foster would be welcomed, there was also concern that the props were playing too many games for them to be at their best in the test matches.

The unfortunate Jack Kitching would automatically be ineligible for the next test, but the tourists – barring a disaster – had ample choice in the backs, except at full-back, which seemed to have a hoodoo.

Many of the players had received more than their share of bruises from which to recover, and none more so than Albert Johnson. As already indicated he had also been the recipient of some very violent play. Besides having to contend with what all the British party were sure was the stiff-arm tackle to end all stiff-arm tackles, he had been bodily thrown off the pitch into the surrounding barriers, landing in the crowd. Certainly, he never drew any attention to the ferocity of the tackling he received, never gave his opponents the satisfaction of thinking they had hurt him and carried on playing as if nothing had happened to upset his game.

The tourists were clearly a very special breed of men, but out on the rugby field they were hardly likely to get much sympathy from the crowd or referees. While the players were hardly enamoured by the standard being set by the Australian referees, there was never an occasion where they objected to any particular official. Nothing on this tour was made easy for them and even the Australian press, which was hardly supportive, was gradually becoming critical of the home authorities, in particular the occasions when the tourists had to arrange their own transport.

Many of the players had just finished six years service in the forces, and now were spending many months away on the other side of the world, leading to further absence from their families and homes. They were very different type from many modern sportsmen, and there were no drunken sprees, bad behaviour or ridiculous demands made by them of the tour management. Whatever problems befell the team they acted together and they were great diplomats for their country.

## The 'biting' incident

The tourists woke up the day after the test match to huge newspaper headlines, which were full of reports about the 'biting' incident between Jorgenson and Kitching. Every Australian newspaper had the incident on its front page, and rarely can rugby league have so dominated the media. This was a story which was going to run and run, no matter how much the authorities tried to diffuse the event.

The match itself was relegated to the inside pages and was of minor importance compared to the dramatic sending off. Both players were due to face the New South Wales rugby league board and give their own individual evidence. Already, the officials of the Australian Rugby League were indicating that there would be a full official enquiry into the whole incident and no stone would be left unturned. Kitching's dismissal meant he would be out of contention for the second test match but, fortunately for the British team, the centre positions had not been affected by injury.

Biting is very rare in rugby league, even in modern times, and any mention of it causes upset – always the intention is to stamp it out. To have these allegations in a test match was bad enough but what was even worse, was that the accused was an Australian and even more, their captain. There were several photographs in the newspapers of Jack Kitching bearing his chest and displaying the purported marks to show that the incident had actually taken place, although none of the pictures gave any conclusive evidence of a bite mark.

However, there was clear evidence that Kitching had sustained an injury to his chest. It could have been a simple bruise, and plenty of

Jack's comrades bore similar evidence, which is all part and parcel of a tough Australian and British encounter and not necessarily a bite mark. This had not been a gentle match to say the least. The reports of the match dealt with the violent incidents in great detail and several of the players were shown in photographs looking as if they had been involved in a major brawl.

Trevor Foster's recollection of the 'biting' incident is interesting. He said in his biography: "Jack was never a dirty player. I remember vividly that they were both on the floor and Jack punched Jorgensen. The referee arrived on the spot and said 'Kitching, off!'... When he got to the dressing room he took off his shirt and pointed at his breast bone. There were bite marks on his chest and that's why he threw the punch."

## The crowd

This test match had been watched by one of the largest crowds ever seen in Australia and there were many stories recounted about the crowd's behaviour, and the number who had required first aid. Fortunately, although there had been many individual incidents, there were few serious injuries. The major problem had been spectators fainting, mainly because of the immense pressure of other spectators jostling them. The other pages covering the match were made up of overhead shots of the crowds packed into the Sydney Cricket Ground and the human swathe that was shown in the ground is really staggering. The SCG over the years had a long history of large crowds for cricket test matches, but never before had held such huge numbers. While the official crowd attendance appears not to be excessive, the invasions through the open members' gate had certainly pushed the number attending the match above the official figure of 64,527. This number has been exceeded since that time, but the cricket members have been included in those totals.

The actual newspaper coverage of play was minimal. In some cases this may have owed much to the restricted views available to the press. All admired McCue and the astute way he had placed his kicks, which had constantly taken the sting out of the Australian attack just has they neared the British tryline. He had employed an extensive kicking game following the dismissal of Jack Kitching, and had showed the experience of a wise old head. This had given his colleagues much needed respite from the constant pressure applied by the Australians. This had been a constant source of irritation to the home team, who had been driven back by these tactics on numerous occasions, and it had certainly prevented a non-stop onslaught being applied on the tourists' last line of defence.

The major concern of the Australian press was the seeming latitude which had been given to Ike Owens, and the way he had been allowed the opportunity to expose weaknesses in the home defence. There was much discussion as to what tactics the Australians should employ to close him down, otherwise the Ashes would be thrown away. When Owens had been operating at loose-forward, prior to the Lions having to change their line up because of the sending off incident, he had been using his exceptional speed to great effect, and all too easily had been able to create openings in the home side's defence. The Australians felt that Owens gave the Lions an added advantage, in that the effect of his play was to give Britain an extra half-back. They then had to face Owens reverting to the role of a hard running forward hitting their defensive line at full force. One reporter went as far as to say that Owens was now Australia's public enemy number one, and until the home nation came up with a feasible plan to stop him, it was very doubtful if Australia could regain the Ashes. All were agreed that if Australia were going to win the series, the Welshman had to be given very little room to operate in. A former Australian captain rated Owens as the fastest forward he had ever seen, and the majority of reporters commented on his astonishing acceleration. The general feeling was that Ike Owens was probably even faster than Johnson and Batten, the British wingers who certainly were not slow.

The Australian writer E.E. Christenson said that Owens and McCue were dominant around the scrums, making the blindside their own territory. However, he felt that if McCue had still had his pre-war speed the Australians would have been thoroughly beaten.

Journalist Tom Goodman speculated on the possibility of a fourth test match following the 8–8 draw at the SCG. However, he felt that a decision would depend on whether the New Zealand leg of the tour went ahead.

Jorgensen was quoted in a number of Australian newspapers saying that he would take legal action over the 'biting' incident, as his good name was being impugned. He also said that Ernest Ward had been involved in the assault by Kitching. However, there is no corroboration of this, as photographs show that Ward was at least 20 to 30 yards away at the time. The threat of legal action was not a path that the Australian management wanted to follow.

Indeed, it was quite clear that the New South Wales Rugby League board now wanted to take the heat away from the biting incident as quickly as possible, and in fact no charges were made against Jorgenson who, in the view of the board did not have to appear before them, because the referee had not cited the Australian captain. Jack Kitching appeared before the board, and their verdict was that the sending off would be considered sufficient punishment considering his unblemished previous playing record.

Kitching also announced to the press that he was not making any accusation against Jorgenson. He hoped very much that the incident could now be forgotten by everyone and that all parties now ensure that the further success of the tour was the main priority. The Lions tour manager George Popplewell, said that they (the Lions), would not be taking this matter any further, and were now looking forward to maintaining good standards which already existed to ensure the future success of the tour.

Unfortunately, the media and of course the public, did not want the matter to drop, which was shown by the vast number of letters received by the newspapers on the subject. So intense and heated was the situation becoming that one of the Sydney papers established a daily 'bite' column, which consisted of a series of cartoons relating to supposedly amusing incidents of individuals facing the perils of biting.

Jack Kitching was a very quiet, unassuming, studious individual, not given to partying. He always acted with impeccable manners, and behaved like a teacher, his off-field profession. He always played the game by the rule book and was a hard, direct-running, centre. In the late 1940s there were a number of matches against the Australian or New Zealand touring parties, and inevitably and coincidentally at Bradford, all of which seemed to become named 'The Battle of Odsal' by the local press. Kitching was conspicuous by not taking any part in any ensuing fracas. He was best known as a mediator who cooled the temperature when troubles started.

While on tour, Kitching had met up with an old friend who was now living in Australia and was a newspaper reporter. This individual was somewhat injudicious in reporting on their friendship, possibly, after stating that Jack was a peaceful man, and indeed such was the reporter's faith in him, that he had chosen him to be his son's godfather. Some of the readers' responses to this article in the newspapers are best forgotten, and Kitching's friend received much abuse for his statement.

The biting incident would just not go away, and every day there were supposed new stories relating to it. The press were still fuelling the debate with cartoons relating to biting and many had very dubious stories and comment on the subject. One newspaper even went on to try and discover the meat butcher who supplied the Australian players.

If the Australian management board thought that Kitching's appearance before them would end the matter or if they shared his wish that this should be forgotten as a topic, they were wrong. It was becoming clear that nothing was being served by pushing the case under the carpet. There was certainly a feeling among a large section of the press that there should be a full enquiry into the whole incident. This cause was further abetted when the match doctor refused to say what the actual cause of Kitching's injury was. He made matters worse when he went on to say that he knew what the actual cause was, and that he would only reveal it if he was called to give evidence at an official enquiry. This statement made the situation even more heated. The New South Wales Rugby League was due to hold a delegates meeting the following day. Many of the delegates were reported in the press as saying that they were determined to raise the matter so that once and for all the air could be cleared.

The ensuing meeting turned out to be an anti-climax, because the board informed those present that they had already carried out its own internal enquiry, which substantially cleared any allegation of biting. A dentist had been called in, who was often a witness in identifying the teeth of individuals for the police and who was sure that Kitching's wound was not a bite mark. He was more than willing to testify to that in a written statement. Kitching himself, the meeting was told, had in his first statement not actually even claimed he had been bitten. They went on to add that he had only raised the matter following the pressure put on him by reporters. However, considering rapid publishing required to get the reports into the newspapers, this seems unlikely to be correct. The board said that the photographs of the 'bite' clearly showed it was a scratch to which iodine had been applied. This had made it appear much worse in the photographs, and the matter had then unfortunately been blown up out of proportion. But how the board could be so sure raised only more doubts, because the majority of newspapers had shown photographs of Kitching's bare chest and no mention had been made of treatment with iodine. Rather strangely, the official match doctor was not asked to make a statement, and was never questioned on the matter by the board on any future occasion.

As the Lions management and Jack Kitching himself no longer wished to pursue the matter, it was decided by the Australian Rugby League that Jorgenson had no case to answer, and little would be served by questioning him about it. He had said many times to various parties that under no circumstances had he bitten his opponent.

Two Australian newsgroups of the time had separate films of the 'biting' incident. These were shot at varying angles, and in those days the only way to view them was to go to the local cinema, because television was not yet established in Australia. Naturally cinemas across Australia were packed with rugby league followers, who were not there to see the major feature film being screened, but wanted to see the match incident. Apparently, one of the companies claimed to have a better view of the incident than its competitor, and to have conclusive evidence concerning the incident. However, the footage was not clear and the claim was almost certainly made to outscore its competitor. Both films were inconclusive. This led to some disturbances at cinemas, particularly if the patrons thought the wrong newsreel was being screened.

On one occasion there was a riot when the local newspaper had printed slide shots of the incident purporting to substantiate the case from one of the newsreels. Unfortunately, the local cinema showed the version which had not been shown in the local newspaper. The cinema had to close for over a week while the damage to its interior could be repaired following the riot which erupted by the patrons who thought they were being cheated.

It seemed as if all the newspapers were now intimating that every violent incident which had occurred during the match was due to the tourists. The Lions must have welcomed one voice of reason from Australian reporter W.F. Corbett. He said that it was about time consideration for England was exhibited, and that the 'knockers' should take the blinkers off their eyes. While there was much talk about the tourists' stiff-arm tackles, easily the worst example was by an Australian, on Albert Johnson's head. Another time an Australian hurtled into Johnson, crashing him on his back and head when the winger was nowhere near the ball.

With all the clamour in the Australian press, it is not surprising that the general public must have thought that the tourists were a side of thugs. But the situation had a lighter side too. An amusing story appeared in the newspapers surrounding an incident which had occurred in Sydney railway station when the tourists were departing for the next stage of the tour. A rather portly gentleman helped an old lady who was struggling with her luggage, into her train compartment. He kindly stacked her cases onto the luggage racks. She thanked him most kindly stating that she had been frightened of meeting the British rugby league side who she had heard were travelling on the same train. The helpful gentleman was, of course, Frank Whitcombe. Throughout the tour there continued to be a love-hate relationship between the Bradford player and the press.

# 6. Queensland

The tourists must have been more than pleased about leaving Sydney. They were hoping to put the 'biting' incident behind them and looking forward to the less torrid waters of Queensland.

Many of the matches there were to take place at venues of which the tourists had probably never heard and where there would not be many sights to see. However, after such a busy schedule so early in the tour and with all the injuries picked up by various players, it seemed certain the party needed a rest. Wilf Gabbatt said in his official report that "The travelling arrangements in Queensland... were also very trying." However, he does acknowledge the assistance of the Queensland Rugby League, saying that the matter was beyond their control. On one trip, their coach was attached to a goods train, resulting in a 12-hour journey instead of seven. He said that after this they tried to travel by air when possible, lifting the players' morale.

However, the players were still expected to visit local people's houses, and be pictured with their babies, and attend special tea parties, almost like politicians trying to gather votes. Official gatherings in public buildings were almost impossible because most of them were unavailable for functions to make fuel savings. Such was Ike Owens's newfound fame and popularity that every day his picture appeared in the papers holding a baby or having an ice cream with local residents.

Some of the matches were to take place in areas where the population was sparse, and many of the spectators had to travel hundreds of miles to attend. The matches were usually based on regional teams rather than local clubs. The Australian government must have been amazed to see how the public were to flout their strict travelling restrictions. Attendance at these matches should have been discouraged, but it was very soon clear that they were being ignored by the public. No one wanted to miss seeing the tourists from the mother country. The government was hardly in a position to complain, after persuading an international side to tour. Without doubt the tour was a great morale booster for the Australian people. The matches were often played in small country grounds which were hardly constructed for the huge numbers who wanted to watch. However, there were no complaints from anyone, and the matches were reported as if they were huge public gatherings of friends and family, which is exactly what they were.

To avoid the travel restrictions, ancient farm carts were brought out, dusted down and used. People from miles around made sure they attended, even using pack mules as transport to get to these special occasions. Doors were opened to complete strangers and, although there were few or no hotels, apparently no one had any difficulty in finding a place to sleep. The match reports are full of the locals struggling to get into the grounds, and then attempting to get a decent view. Very often the judicious placing of farm carts as stands sufficed, allowing the fans could get an improved view. A very popular observation place appeared to have been on top of the stand roofs, and very few match reports fail to report an incident of supporters sustaining injury after falling from them.

The start of one match had to be delayed for over half an hour, because the stand roof totally collapsed, because of the weight of the spectators who were standing on it. The report shows little interest in how many spectators were injured, but concentrates more on how quickly the locals could clear the debris and provide room for spectators so they could watch the match as soon as possible.

The first match following the first test was against a side representing Northern New South Wales. It was the last in that state prior to moving onto Queensland. Fortunately for the Lions, Joey Jones had made a rapid recovery and took over the problem full-back position. The backs were completely changed to give a rest to those who had played in the test match, but injuries had now struck the forwards. Only Curran who had not played in the test was available and fit to give any relief to his colleagues. The news was bad for Fred Hughes, who would be out for over a month. Sadly Trevor Foster was also showing no signs of any improvement.

It was feared that Martin Ryan, the other full-back, would be out for the rest of the Australian part of the tour. However, he joined up with the touring party when his condition allowed.

The forwards, although badly in need of a rest, were given little respite. Joe Egan, usually a hooker, moved into the second row, along with George Curran, who was ostensibly the cover for Egan. While neither normally played in this position, it was very much a case of needs must. George Popplewell, the tour manager, instructed both Owens and Egan to avoid unnecessary tackles, and to pass the ball to the backs as soon as possible.

Egan appears to have taken little notice of these instructions and enjoyed his new role to such an extent that he scored a first-half hat-trick. Many knowledgeable spectators remarked that his first-half performance was one of the best displays of second row play seen at the ground. The tour manager must have given him a stiff talking to at the interval, because his second-half display was well below the standard of his first. Incidentally Joe's club colleague Ken Gee took on the specialist position of hooker, and ensured that the tourists were dominant in the scrums.

This match was played at Tamworth, and many of the spectators had travelled more than 350 miles to get there. The attendance was 7,270, with receipts of £804, which was extremely good for such a remote area. Indeed, the travelling restrictions had not prevented a ground record being established. The Lions had had another overnight train trip to get to the game.

The tourists could not complain about the warmth of their welcome, which was always first class. Certainly the residents of the outback showed how much they valued the visit of the tourists.

The tourists were soon on top and at half time led 38–0. The final score was 61–5, with the Lions scoring 13 tries and 11 goals. The loudest cheer of the day, however, was when the home side scored their converted try. The home side had been unlucky, as they hit the crossbar twice with penalties and had two tries disallowed.

Some of the tourists took the opportunity to show some open exhibition play. Owens did some spectacular runs which thrilled the crowd, and Joe Egan was not slow in showing his colleagues that he could perform dummies with the best of them. Ted Ward took on the goalkicking duties and showed that the tourists had a good kicker as back up. He converted 10 tries, kicked a penalty, and showed the skills that would very soon make him British rugby league's top goalkicker for two successive seasons. The full list of try scorers was: Joe Egan with three, Bassett, Knoweldon and Lewthwaite with two each, and Owens, Jones, Phillips, and Davies who all contributed one.

After the game, George Popplewell was pleased that all the forwards who had played had come through unscathed. There was also better news concerning Fred Hughes, who appeared to be making a faster recovery than expected. If this was maintained, the selection group would have at least eight forwards to choose from, instead of the uninjured forwards effectively picking themselves.

The next game was certainly going to be hard because the tourists were scheduled to play the Queensland state select side, who were determined to outshine their rival state of New South Wales. Certainly, Queensland thought they were under-represented in the selection of the national side and hoped that to defeat the tourists would help press claims for test selection of their players. The Lions had an overnight train trip, and arrived in Brisbane at 8pm on 20 June. Doug Phillips recalls sharing a hotel room with four other players.

Despite more players becoming available, the tourists' injury crisis was still problematic and when the giant prop Frank Whitcombe faced Queensland, he had played nine matches without a break. He was playing two matches per week which was taking a very heavy toll. The effort clearly had a telling effect on him because his weight dropped from 17½ stone to 16½ stone. Yet, nobody could see any notable loss in his tremendous appetite. The Australians nicknamed him 'Ironsides' as a mark of respect, a name which stuck for the rest of the tour.

The Queensland match was awaited eagerly by the Australian public. The tourists still had a problem in selecting a pack. Whoever was chosen, it was clear that one or two of the forwards would be carrying injuries. Owens was the major doubt. He had strained his Achilles tendon, and had an infection on the side of his knee. He was unable to participate in the final training sessions. Tommy McCue was also unavailable, due to a late injury he had sustained in the first test match which had affected his shoulder. It was impossible for him to raise his arm, but he hoped to be fully recovered for the second test.

Herb Steinohrt, a veteran Queensland Kangaroo front-row forward, and the captain of the 1932 Australia side, had seen both the tourists' matches against New South Wales and the first test. More pertinently he was coach to the Queensland side, and would be in charge of Australia for the forthcoming second test. He declared that Owens was the greatest loose-forward he had ever set eyes on, and his plan of action was to keep Owens as quiet as possible if he was fit to play. He said that while it would be disappointing for the crowd if Owens did not play, his task of training a winning side would be made easier.

In the end, there was widespread jubilation throughout the state as Queensland outdid New South Wales in beating the Lions 25–24, although there was only one point in it and the Lions missed a simple conversion. However, that was not going to stop the Queenslanders celebrating beating the all conquering tourists.

The Lions, not surprisingly, gave a lacklustre performance, although this does not take anything away from the home side's efforts. The Queensland pack exerted enough pressure to get on top of the Lions' forwards, and some of their passing also left much to be desired. The passing was so telegraphed at times that Len Kenny, the Queensland winger, must have thought it was his birthday. He made a number of interceptions which, in the second half, enabled Queensland to build up a comfortable lead.

Despite their poor performance, the Lions managed to lead 11–10 at half-time, but in the second half the tourists' strength around the scrums was to turn against them. Kenny picked up a long pass by Owens as he was attempting to catch the Queenslanders off guard and, after a quick passing move, and good backing up, the home side scored. Kenny then intercepted another loose pass – from Jenkins this time – who had been attempting to release Johnson into an opening in the Australian defence. This left Kenny with an uninterrupted run to the tourists' tryline. The Lions' biggest failure was Risman's kicking, which was well off target, and appeared to be a continuation of his abysmal form in the first test.

The Queensland goalkicker, Gayler, managed to kick five goals, while Risman kicked three goals but never looked comfortable with the kicking role.

Queensland scoring against the Lions. (DP)

The Lions defending against Queensland. (DP)

Ike Owens chases a loose ball, with Dai Jenkins on the ground
against Queensland. (DP)

Frank Whitcombe, Ken Gee, Les White and Doug Phillips
defending against Queensland. (DP)

A visit to the Lone Pine Gardens in Brisbane on 23 June.

Top: Feeding Kangaroos. (DP)

Middle: Doug Phillips being kissed by a wallaby, with Owens, Knowelden, Horne and Lewthwaite watching. (DP)

Bottom: Making friends with Koalas. (DP)

After half time, Queensland built up a 25–11 lead. The visitors were submerged by the home side's pack which was now in full control. Then the tourists stirred themselves, and staged a magnificent fightback with only 15 minutes left. Batten and Johnson led the way with tries, and the Lions managed to cut the lead down to only one point. The final kick of the match was Risman's attempt to convert Johnson's try from underneath the posts. Sadly, it was not the skipper's day, and he somehow sliced his kick. The ball passed outside the upright and, while the tourists were left to think what might have been, the home crowd went home in a mood of ecstasy. This was enhanced by the knowledge that they had achieved what New South Wales had failed to accomplish.

Risman and the tourists were not slow to congratulate Queensland on their win, although they were more relieved that this tough match had not resulted in anymore serious injuries.

Following this match, the tourists' management group met to discuss what could be done to help relieve their overworked forwards from their non-stop schedule of play. They had only seven fit forwards, and most of them had played five matches in 20 days. Certainly this was a situation that could not be allowed to continue, and it also showed that the original tour selection, with 11 forwards, had underestimated the demands of the trip.

Risman put himself forward to play in the second-row, but the general feeling was that he would be better placed to control match tactics more readily in the backs. The compromise reached was that Ted Ward would now play regularly in the second row. There was general relief that the remaining matches before the second test were not too demanding. This was partly because a Queensland side was playing a New South Wales side as a trial match prior to the second test. This would help ensure that the quality of opposition players in the local games would not be too strong.

The tourists had to play another four matches prior to the second test. Despite the setback of losing to Queensland, the Lions resolved to ensure that they would not lose any of these remaining matches.

The next game was three days after the Queensland game, in Bundaberg. It was a hard-fought match against Wide Bay, who were determined to show their own supporters that they were as good as the tourists, with muscle to match. Despite the home side having the assistance of a friendly referee, the locals were beaten 16–12. The following three matches were against sides who were willing, but did not have enough skill to run the tourists close. This enabled the Lions to come through with only one more major injury.

It took the Lions 13 hours by train to get to Rockhampton, a distance of 179 miles. On Thursday 27 June, a comfortable 35–12 win was achieved against Central Queensland in Rockhampton. The half-back partnership of Willie Davies and Dai Jenkins was much too fast and composed for their opponents. But once again, Joey Jones was injured, and now the need to settle the full-back spot was once more a pressing problem for the tourists. It was decided that Ernest Ward would take over the full-back role. He looked to be fit and well again following his injury sustained in the first test, which had led to fluid gathering on his knee.

Although the Lions won easily, a worry note was the poor goalkicking form of Risman and Ted Ward. Both seemed to have lost their usual confidence, and it was decided that Ernest Ward would start the next game as the goalkicker.

Prior to the match, a massive crowd had assembled in the ground, and the previous attendance record was easily beaten. To accommodate all the supporters, even the grandstand roof was packed. As the teams entered the field, someone fell from the roof. The start of the game was delayed until this unfortunate spectator could be taken on a stretcher to hospital. There is no record as to whether he recovered from his injuries.

Gus Risman, in his autobiography, *Rugby Renegade*, published in 1958, recalled his visit to Rockhampton for reasons other than the comfortable win over the local side. He said that the town had hosted many American troops during the war and the hotels had not been restored. The party were in two hotels, and in his he found "the wallpaper hanging in strips from the walls, the bed was rickety and the sheets were in shreds." He went to bed, but then heard shouting. Eric Batten had lifted a seat in the corridor and found it crawling with bugs. Frank Whitcombe was asleep in a bed in the corridor, which collapsed. The next morning they moved to another hotel. Doug Phillips described the hotel he was in as "filthy". Wilf Gabbatt's report coyly notes that "On one occasion in Queensland it was found desirable to transfer the players from a hotel to alternative accommodation."

The match against Central Queensland was followed three days later by an even larger win, 55–16 in Townsville against Northern Queensland. The 7,567 crowd for this game broke the stadium attendance record, as was common throughout the tour. The receipts were £1,298. The trip from Rockhampton to Townsville had been another overnight one, this time without sleeping cars.

All the players had a comfortable work-out, and most pleasing of all for the tourists was Ernest Ward's performance in the troublesome full-back position. He showed he had excellent pace to cover unexpected breakaways and, best of all, throughout the game showed he had an excellent positional sense, which is vital for a full-back.

The party then flew from Townsville to Mackay for the next match on Tuesday 2 July, becoming the first Lions touring team to use this form of transport.

Ward dispelled all doubts about the full-back position against Mackay, and to put icing on the cake, kicked 17 goals in a 94–0 win. It was the final match before the second test. This was an added bonus for the Lions, given Risman's recent poor goalkicking form. Jim Lewthwaite, who was to become a great Cumberland icon, scored seven tries. Lewthwaite did not play in any of the tests, but proved himself to be a very capable winger. Throughout the tour he contested with Batten the position of the tourists' leading try scorer. Incidentally, the match was played before another record crowd of 5,044.

The one disappointing feature after the match was that the tourists had to face an overnight train journey without the comfort of sleeping berths. They were due to arrive in Brisbane three days before the test match, while their Australian opponents were given the benefit of having a full week's rest. Apparently there had been the opportunity of air travel, but this time the managers decided not to fly, and the opportunity of giving the players a much-needed rest was lost.

Then, of course, it was once more time to get ready for the match, which the whole of the rugby league fraternity in Australia wished to see. Extra excitement was in the air after the tourists' recent defeat against Queensland. The majority of Australian pundits were now writing off the Lions as a major threat. There was one dissenting voice, the journalist George Thatcher, who declared that the British were at their most dangerous when they had drawn you into thinking that they were at their weakest, and that recent history suggested that once again Australia could be facing a sucker punch. Still, he was a lone voice, and this was the time when Australia could strike back. Who wants to listen to dissenting voices when your national side appears to be in the ascendancy?

Although there was a national transport strike due to be held on the day of the match, there was little doubt that no true staunch Australian was going to miss their national side put the Poms to the sword. Certainly hopes and aspirations were high, and Queensland were now considered good enough to supply five players to the Australian side. The whole nation expected the old enemy to be well and truly routed and, if Queensland were unfortunate not to have had more players selected, at least the victory would be on their soil.

# 7. The second test

Despite coal shortages restricting public transport, the government-imposed travelling restrictions and a public transport national strike, no one was going to be put off from trying to get to this crucial match. Many queued all night and there were many small camping sites by all the gates. Anyone who had any kind of transport found themselves expected to give both friends, neighbours, and all and sundry a lift, Many thousands walked miles to get there, and by early morning hundreds of people were thronging the whole area outside the stadium all trying to gain entry to the Brisbane Exhibition Ground. The gates were opened at 7am.

By late morning, the police were left with no option but to close all the gates. This was despite the fact that all the roads to the ground were blocked solid with people and all types of transport and, as far distant as the eye could see, there was a solid army of people making their way to the venue. The decision to close the gates was not a popular one and caused general unrest with the fans still outside the ground. So enraged did people become that the police were faced with a massive charge by the crowd, who were desperate to gain entry. The surging throng was successful with this initial push, and it was estimated that there were easily 10,000 gatecrashers.

In an attempt to control a situation which was fast approaching anarchy, extra police reinforcements were summoned, and at last some kind of order was restored. Unfortunately the ground covered seven acres, and was established for cricket. There were several open areas away from the direct playing area where there were exhibition stands for a forthcoming agricultural show and cricket practice areas. The police were faced with the very difficult task of supervising all these open areas, and it was possible for more gatecrashers to get in to the ground despite all the extra police surveillance.

To make matters worse for the police, while all this pandemonium was going on, the Australian side arrived, after driving round the ground for 20 minutes. So bad was the pressure on the outside gates that at first only half the team could gain entrance. More police had to be called to the team entrance, so that the rest of the Australian squad could get in. Unfortunately the pressure on this gate became so bad that the last few remaining members of the side had to be escorted away to other entrances, and after a hectic hour they were at last able to make their way to the dressing rooms.

The Lions were comfortably ensconced in their hotel and were blissfully unaware of the scenes which were taking place at the playing ground. Fortunately, Harry Sunderland, who was travelling with the team, had the good sense to get in contact with the local authorities to check what was happening, and also to find out what time the tourists should arrive at the ground.

It was quite clear that the congestion was so bad that there was no way that the Lions could get through the massive congestion under their own steam. The only solution to this, which was fast becoming an intractable situation, was to provide a police escort for the party all the way to the ground. As it was, the tourists' arrival was very likely to encourage gatecrashers to attempt to get in alongside the players.

Harry Sunderland was an individual who always seemed to know everyone and, when all else failed, he had an amazing ability to get things done, however impossible it first appeared. He had originally been a rugby league administrator. However, his rugby league reports brought him to prominence, and he became one of the game's most respected writers. He contacted the police chief to arrange an escort.

The first response Sunderland received was not very encouraging. The police chief said there were enough people in the ground already, without attempting to get any more in. This remark may have been Australian humour, because if the tourists were not to arrive for the match, then there is no doubt that there would have been a riot, with all its repercussions.

The problem was solved when a number of cars formed a single line to carry the players, and then police formed alongside as outriders, like a presidential cavalcade. Every available policeman was on duty, and the police overtime budget must have gone through the roof. After much pushing and shoving along the route the tourists finally gained entry to the ground.

The actual attendance for the test match was the largest ever for Brisbane, although the official figure of 40,500 does not reflect this. The newspaper banner headlines quote 45,000 spectators, 5,000 members, plus 10,000 gatecrashers. The official attendance is now listed as a less than the ground record but, of course, the members, and gatecrashers are not included in that total. To put this in context, the attendances in Brisbane for the Lions test matches in 1932 and 1936 did not top 30,000.

The ground was so overcrowded, that the spectators spilled out onto the touchlines. The British support squad and their Australian counterparts were on opposite sides of the field surrounded by the spectators. There were also many unofficial transfers going on between enclosures within the ground, and one budding entrepreneur charged spectators to come through a gap in the fence into another part of the ground. Such was the pressure in their enclosure that the supporters were more than happy to make the payment, and with the ease in crowd pressure were probably pleased to pay it.

The week after the match, the Queensland Agricultural Show was due to be held at the ground. All the trade stands were completely stripped by the spectators, who used any available item to help them to have a better standing view. A group of spectators was able to salvage a 20-foot wooden plank, and place it on drums to give them a better vantage point. Even the would-be spectators outside the ground had not finished attempting to gain entrance. Many of them threw ropes over the branches of trees in an attempt to haul themselves over the outer walls of the ground.

## The teams

There were a number of changes to the Lions side from the first test. Ernest Ward, normally a centre, duly took over the troublesome full-back role. Clearly, he had impressed everyone in the previous games. His goalkicking had been so successful that it was also decided that he would take over that onerous responsibility. Gus Risman, who had been less than happy in the first test in the position of full-back, now switched back to his usual centre role – here his declining speed would not be so exposed. Alongside him was Wigan's Ted Ward in his usual centre position. Eric Batten, who had an outstanding match in the first test, had picked up a thigh strain, which affected his running. He was replaced by the Halifax winger Arthur Bassett who, at the age of 30, was making his test debut. Bassett had played international rugby for Wales in the union code. Although there had been grave doubts over the fitness of Ike Owens, it was felt that with strong strapping to a troublesome leg injury he would prevail, and though his speed may be affected, his all-round play and strong defensive tackling would be a major influence. Just his presence was a psychological factor which would certainly disturb the Australians.

The 'biting' incident which had caused so much conflict in the first test, was somewhat diffused, in that Canterbury's Ron Bailey had taken the place of Joe Jorgenson as Australian captain. The unfortunate Kitching, of course, had a one-match test ban. At loose-forward, Noel Mulligan was injured, and was replaced by Newcastle's Jack Hutchinson for his only international appearance.

The Australian press was all now agreed that, if the open play could be kept away from Owens, then Australia had an excellent opportunity to win. Certainly, if he was allowed to make his strong surging runs at the home defence, as he had in the first test, then the Australians would be in trouble, particularly as they had appeared powerless to control the combination of Horne, McCue and Owens which was the springboard of the tourists' attack.

L.H. Kearney wrote in the Australian *Courier-Mail* that "...to beat England in the second test today, Australia must bank on passing speed to combat England's ruggedness and devastating spoiling tactics. It will be fatal to Australia's chances to become embroiled in a battering-ram, man-to-man struggle. I have yet to see an Australian team triumph over England in the traditional forward game from Jimmy Lomas's team in 1910 to James Brough's team in 1936."

The team line-ups were as follows:

*Australia:* Dave Parkinson, Edgar Newham, Ron Bailey ( c ), Joe Jorgenson, Lionel Cooper, Pat Devery, John Grice, Frank Farrell, George Watt, Ray Westaway, Arthur Clues, Reg Kay, Jack Hutchinson.

*Great Britain:* Ernest Ward, Arthur Bassett, Ted Ward, Gus Risman ( c ), Albert Johnson, Willie Horne, Tommy McCue, Ken Gee, Joe Egan, Frank Whitcombe, Les White, Doug Phillips, Ike Owens.

*Referee:* S.W. Chambers

The national anthem prior to the match was lost in a cacophony of noise, mainly drowned out by supporters shouting for others to sit down. Surprisingly, the match actually started on time, but the first time the ball went over the touchline, the referee stopped the game and had the touchline areas cleared of spectators. This held up play for five minutes. The British support staff took the chance to cross the field, and were able to take up a safer position near to their opponents' bench – previously they had been right on the very edge of the touchline. It still only needed an overzealous tackle, and a player would be tumbling on top of them.

Following the first test, the Australians had decided that Gus Risman was the weak link, and they would be able to cause problems exploiting his lack of mobility. Unfortunately for them, there is a vast difference in having one's lack of pace exploited when playing full-back, and playing at centre. This policy proved to be mistaken, and when Risman was heavily tackled the first time he gathered the ball, the Australians found out what a strong and masterful player Risman was. The captain had a reputation as one of the hardest tacklers in the British game, and that afternoon his opponents found out how he had earned that reputation. Jorgenson and Bailey, the Australian centres, must have wondered what had happened, as they spent the rest of the afternoon receiving a master class in the art of centre play. They were constantly grounded by the British skipper who was more than ably backed up by Ted Ward. Risman's performance was so effective that after the game the Australian press wholeheartedly asserted that he gave one of the best ever displays of centre play seen in Australia.

The British camp's concern that the heavy strapping would slow his speed proved to be groundless as Ike Owens, on receiving the ball from the first scrum, broke away from the ensuing melee on the halfway line, and had the Australian defence all at sea. He showed that Australia were no nearer to solving the problem of how to control him. He sold a number of dummies before he finally passed to McCue, leaving him with the line wide open. Unfortunately the half-back was unable to keep hold of the ball and the home supporters breathed a

74

general sigh of relief, as more by luck than actual good defence, the tourists had failed to score.

Unfortunately for the Australians, this was only a warning signal of more dangers to come and they could not relax, if the powerful Welshman, who was proving to be such a thorn in their side, gained possession of the ball.

Britain's ploy of using Owens as an attacking force clearly unsettled the home side. It was evident that when the tourists won the ball from a scrum, the Australians were always unsure as to where the Lions' main point of the attack would be directed. Fortunately for the Australians, unlike in the first test, they were gaining more possession from the scrums. While they were not able to put the same pressure on the tourists when in possession of the ball, at least they were not in danger of having their defence being constantly probed by their opponents.

Play was unsettled for a long period, and any open play was impossible, with some of the players of both sides attempting to settle old scores from previous games. There were a number of incidents which required the referee's intervention. It was quite apparent that both sides were more than ready to involve themselves in fisticuffs should the occasion arise. Australia, with their dominance of possession from the scrimmages, came close to the British line on a number of occasions. However, the tourists' defence, superbly marshalled by Risman, was able to deal with all attacks very safely. The nearest Australia came to scoring was a quick breakaway by the flying winger Lionel Cooper. He made 30 yards in a superb, powerful burst, and was very unfortunate not to have any of his colleagues backing him up. His attempt came to a halt with three British defenders making sure that the attack was smothered out.

After just over 15 minutes play, the impasse was finally broken. Once again, the tourists were able to use their mastery behind the scrums to devastating effect. McCue took the ball from the scrum, went round the blind side and sold two outrageous dummies to his opponents. The Australians kept hanging back and appeared to be certain he would switch play to the open side, so failed to fully cover the danger. Horne suddenly appeared and joined McCue on the blind side, while many of the Australian defenders moved to the open side, where Owens was lurking, and clearly expected the ball to be switched to him ready for one of his surges. McCue then made a short kick to Bassett, who had moved inside, and there was no defender in position to stop the flying Halifax winger. Bassett scored what must have been one of the easiest tries of his career. The conversion attempt by Ernest Ward from the touchline just missed. It was surprising that Ward could even manage to get close as he had to step through spectators as he addressed the ball. It was first blood to the British but it was clear that a single try would not resolve this titanic struggle.

The power of the Australian attack was somewhat diminished. Ernest Ward had the beating of his opposite number Dave Parkinson, which meant that the home side had to provide extra cover in their defence, and Parkinson was unable to back up their attacking play. Even so, the Australians mounted an attack on the British blind side, no doubt working on the theory that what the Lions could do, they could do better. By the time Cooper received the ball he must have thought he had run into a brick wall, as the British defenders were massed to meet him. The play then was fairly evenly mixed and also contained a number of fiery outbreaks, all penalised, but there did not appear enough evidence of severe malpractice for the referee to send any one off.

Ken Gee and Les White were involved in a number of punch-ups, with Clues leading the way for the Australians. Despite also being a policeman, there was certainly no reluctance on Clues's part to become involved in a number of affrays. From one such incident, Joe Jorgenson attempted to convert a penalty from 40 yards out and near the touchline, but his effort missed.

Shortly before half-time, Ernest Ward was able to convert a penalty from just over 30 yards and wide out. This followed two brilliant bursts by the tourists. First, Owens again had the Australian defence all at sea, but unfortunately McCue knocked on. This was followed by Horne and Johnson combining splendidly, and this led to obstruction by the Australians, leading to Ward's successful penalty. There were now glimpses of the tourists getting on top, with Owens making two great runs at the Australian defence, which were only just stopped.

Added to this, Dave Parkinson, the Australian full-back, was having a dreadful match and dropped two balls very near his own line. The defenders were somewhat fortunate to scramble the ball out of play before any of the tourists could get to it. To be fair, the margin of the Lions' 5–0 lead could have been reduced just before the break. Jorgenson had a penalty from a reasonable distance, and almost directly in front of the posts, but missed.

The tourists, despite being behind 19–17 on the scrum count, and 7–2 on penalties, had been on top. They had caused the Australians defence many problems with clever flick passes and Owens had been able to break quickly from the scrums, a ploy which had distracted the Australian defence. There was everything to play for in the second half, and the next try would be crucial.

**The second half**

The second half started very much as the first half had finished, with Joe Jorgenson kicking at goal, following a penalty conceded by Ken

Gee, but this time he was successful. This reduced the Lions' lead to 5–2. The home side were heartened by a devastating run from Cooper, who nearly broke through after beating two defenders but was wrapped up by the tourists' cover defence. The crowd was now in full voice, and for once they glimpsed a chance for their side at last to beat England. Another burst against the visitors' line almost led to Ray Westaway scoring, but once again the tourists' defence stood resolute. Certainly, the home side had come out for the second half determined to eradicate the tourists lead. Such was their mood and confidence, that Jorgenson, instead of kicking at goal when he had a reasonable chance to score, kicked the ball into touch by the defenders' line hoping his team would win the resulting scrum. All the opening pressure was by the Australians who were desperate to score.

However, Owens intercepted an Australian passing movement and made a devastating run up the field, which gave the Lions the opportunity to attack the Australian line. The tourists had ridden out the early storm and now had the bit between their teeth. Owens showed his best when making two devastating bursts at the Australians, who were very fortunate to survive this new onslaught. The first run ended almost on the Australian tryline, with the ball running loose, and a forward pass prevented a score with the line open. The sigh of relief from the home supporters could be heard inside and outside the ground.

The tourists were not to be denied, however, and McCue worked the blindside once again from a scrum near the Australian line. Almost in an identical rerun of the first try, McCue and Horne combined to create an opening large enough for Bassett to squeeze in at the corner flag. Alfred Drewry reported that the winger "flashed in to finish a prearranged blindside move by Horne and McCue which left the Australian defence standing." Bassett must have been surprised at how easy it was to score tries at this level, because in scoring both his tries not an Australian hand had been laid upon him. Ernest Ward had to step into the crowd once more in order to take the conversion, and it was no surprise that again he failed.

Although this try was a blow to the home team, it was also the spur they needed to put even more impetus into their game, and find even deeper reserves to once again take the attack into the tourists' half. With the roar of the crowd behind them they went all out to attack the British defence and, 10 minutes after the Lions' score, they worked the ball across the British line enabling Lionel Cooper to have a direct run for the corner. He did this with devastating effect and, dragging both Ernest and Ted Ward with him, crossed the line to score. It was the sort of try he would repeat very often with his future club, Huddersfield. Needless to say the try was unconverted, as Jorgenson had to contend with the same problem that befell Ernest Ward. Even the Australian supporters on the edge of the field could not move to allow the Australian a decent approach to his conversion attempt.

As the match approached its last 10 minutes, the Lions were showing their undoubted superiority, but what the home nation lacked in skill they more than compensated for with their total commitment. Both Risman and Jorgenson failed with drop-goal attempts and both sides then attempted to drive straight over the try line, a tactic used whenever either came close to the last line of defence.

The deciding move arrived suddenly. Following another defence relieving run by Owens, he swiftly moved the ball out to Johnson, who went on to score the try of the match. He received the ball on the halfway line, and broke away from two defenders by punting it forward. Alfred Drewry described his try as "remarkable", saying that he "juggled with the ball above his head for fully 15 yards before getting it under control and at the same time beat two defenders." He took a flying dive for the line and scored, despite the attentions of Devery who attempted to tackle him. Not surprisingly, Ernest Ward failed to convert from the touchline. The Lions now led 11–5, so the Australians needed to score twice.

The tourists were not finished, however. Ted Ward sprinted downfield, having been put through by Phillips. He went towards the right wing and put Bassett in for his third try, a remarkable achievement on his debut. Bassett was surrounded by his colleagues, congratulating him on his amazing try scoring achievement.

Although the home crowd had become somewhat muted, the Australians were refusing to accept defeat and geared themselves up for a final all-out surge at the British line. From the resultant Australian kick off, the home side raced forward to throw everything into the attack. Ernest Ward, who caught the ball, was over-energetically tackled by Arthur Clues. While he was lying on the ground, he appeared to be the recipient of a rabbit punch. Although the referee and linesman were well placed to see the incident, they appeared totally ignorant of what had occurred. So incensed was the British hooker, Joe Egan, at the lack of official action, that he ran in from more than 20 yards away, and hit Clues with an uppercut which many a professional fighter would have been proud of. It was an uncharacteristic action by the easy going Wigan player, who was heard to mutter "If the referee won't do his job, then someone has to". Egan then showed some common sense by not heading for the players' tunnel following his inevitable sending off, but instead sitting with the British official contingent who were on the touchline – no doubt strength in numbers being the wise option.

Bassett's try had made the final score 14–5 to the Lions. In the second half, Britain had gained a slight advantage in the scrum, although the home side had benefited from a 9–2 penalty count.

Second test action: Owens (left) and Johnson tackling the Australians. (DP)

The crowd at the second test in Brisbane. (DP)

This victory gave the Lions the Ashes, and continued 25 years' domination over Australia, who had last won a series in 1920. The Lions now had the opportunity to go through the test series unbeaten, and become the first side to do this in an Ashes series. Alfred Drewry said that "There was no questioning England's superiority."

The final outcome would now depend very much on the injury count, and how well the players could respond to the tour's demanding playing schedule. They could not relax too much, knowing the Ashes were retained, because the Australians would be more determined than ever to finish with a win.

As he came off the field, Gus Risman gave a short address which was gracious in victory, congratulating the Australians on playing with such determination, giving their all and for their fast rugby. He added that they had been unfortunate not to get the breaks which the Lions had enjoyed.

There was no doubt that the Australian side had given everything that they had, but at times lacked the finesse of the Lions. The British tour manager, Walter Popplewell echoed his captain's comments, and stated that the match had been an excellent advertisement for the game, that the play all through the series had been end-to-end, and probably in the final reckoning Britain had been slightly the better side.

The Australians were not so reserved and stated that their game was still behind the British version. The Australian coach, Herb Steinohrt, said that he admired the Lions' control of the ball which no doubt came from playing on muddy grounds. Even though the Australians had once again lost the Ashes, there was a general agreement that the second test had been an excellent match. With play moving from end-to-end of the pitch, the spectators had seen a very open game. Yes, it had been tough, and no quarter had been given by either side, but Australia was still lacking the essential skills which the British side possessed, and had been essential in their win.

The main Australian reporters concluded after the game that, for the first time on this tour, both packs had been equal, with the Australian forwards getting more of the ball from the scrums than their British counterparts. Unfortunately, the Australians had met two confidence tricksters who were at the top of their form. First, McCue had sold them dummies galore, while Owens had run and then handed out more dummies like a millionaire giving tips. What was most galling was that backs of the calibre of Devery, Bailey and Jorgenson had swallowed them so completely. W.F. Corbett said that Australia had to "trap" Owens to win the third test, as this would be the only way that Australia could blunt England's scoring moves on the blind side.

R.W. Reid in the Australian *Daily Telegraph* wrote that "It was a triumph for England's old men", saying that McCue had played a dominant role behind England's pack, Gus Risman had blocked

Australian moves with his devastating tackles and Arthur Bassett had been perfect in his positional play.

The press wanted Ike Owens to comment on the game, as the Lions' outstanding player, but he turned that compliment aside, saying that McCue had been the brains behind the victory, and deserved all the glory going, adding how well Bassett had done to score a hat-trick on his debut.

Tom Goodman, the famous Australian rugby league journalist, said that "For the ninth consecutive series of tests spread over 25 years Australia has had to leave the rugby league Ashes in England's hands. There have been many contributing factors, but I believe a fairly general explanation is that English players, as a result of their education in their hard school of professional football, have been better equipped for big matches."

Despite the huge attendance and the attempts to gatecrash the match, there were no reports of serious crowd injuries. The only complaints were from several ladies who had snagged their nylons in the crush. While not newsworthy today, in 1946 nylon stockings were precious, and usually obtained from American servicemen.

Of course there was a general air of depression among Australian rugby league followers, who had now gone since 1920 without witnessing an Ashes victory, like British supporters today who have not seen a series win since 1970, a test series win appeared to be a distant dream. This general depression was made worse, because so many of the Australian supporters had used their precious petrol ration getting to and from the match. They could now only hope for a consolation victory in the final test at Sydney, and also hope that the right playing formation could be found. Australia would then have a springboard for success in the future. Perhaps one consolation was the ages of the tourists, because the Lions would also face having to search for new talent in the years ahead.

The main task of the tourists was now completed – they had retained the Ashes after only two test matches but, such was their team spirit, they did not contemplate losing as an option. Trevor Foster later said that they had always been confident of winning, and never thought that Australia could beat them in a test series. Bassett was now the hero of the hour after his hat-trick of tries, and was allowed to sit in the Governor's chair in the Australian Parliament, just for the press photographers. He was not allowed to be in charge of any new government legislation, however...

His main honour, certainly as far as the Welsh were concerned, was to conduct the Welsh choir at its next engagement, which was on local radio. Ike Owens later said that Bassett had completed a special first within the annals of Welsh male voice choirs; he was the first conductor to have a black eye.

81

## The press

Many in the press were now becoming very critical of the way the ARL board had treated the tourists, and labelled their management as 'Abbot and Costello style', after two popular American comedians of the time. They blamed the board for the delay at Fremantle, which had been aggravated by a hold up at Perth, prior to their overland travel to Sydney. They also now accused the board of not arranging transport for the tourists on their arrival in Sydney. Strangely, at the time, the British management had complained bitterly about this but the press seemed uninterested in the tourists' travel problems.

It is rather a pity that the managers of the British touring party had formerly been reticent in making complaints. They had held back because they were aware of post-war conditions and so did not wish to draw attention to the treatment that the touring party had received. But now the media were criticising the Australian board which included complaints about the tourists' arduous itinerary.

Much of this criticism followed a misleading press disclosure about captain Gus Risman and Jack Kitching who had been booked into stay at a better hotel than the rest of the touring party. This story received widespread coverage and, of course the Australians were quick to use it to attack the English class system. They said that the captain and Kitching, who was a teacher, were seen as higher class than their comrades. In fact, Kitching was not the only teacher in the party, and the two players had stayed at a separate hotel because of the ineptitude of the ARL. They had miscalculated the number of tourists, and Risman and Kitching had agreed to be separated from the main group. The press had used a little poetic licence with the story, and had attempted to imply that the hotel where the tourists was booked was not a good enough standard for the other two players, who were themselves incensed at this story.

Risman describes an incident in *Rugby Renegade*, when he and Kitching went to a different hotel to have breakfast with a friend of Risman's who was staying there. He says that there were "other scare stories, and although they were untrue they had an unsettling effect on the whole party."

In his tour report, Wilf Gabbatt said that "Certain members of the Australian press on several occasions caused concern amongst the players by the publishing of alleged remarks they had made during interviews. This also applied to your managers. Eventually at a meeting the players were directed to refrain from making statements, in view of the distortion placed upon their remarks. From my personal observation I am of the opinion that the hospitality given to sections of the team by members of the Australian press was not in the best interests of the players concerned."

# 8. Unbeaten in the Ashes

Before returning to Sydney for the final test match, the tourists had another fortnight on the road, with four more matches.

Schedules were strict and a typical itinerary from the tour is shown below, covering the period after the second test was played.

**Tour itinerary: 6 to 15 July**
*Saturday* after the second test at Brisbane there is an evening invitation to a dance at the City Hall, the dance at the Ritz Ballroom being cancelled because of the lighting restrictions. [This problem would affect a number of functions to which the tourists would in normal times have been invited.]
*Sunday* is by private car transport to the South Coast beaches, as guests of the Queensland Government, on return the party can rest.
*Monday* was a civic reception by the Lord Mayor at the City Hall. Then in the afternoon to attend Parliament House as guests of the Queensland Government.
*Tuesday* to play against the Brisbane team at the Brisbane Cricket Ground.
*Wednesday* to be a [well deserved] free day for all the tourists.
*Thursday* in the morning to travel to Ipswich. Play Ipswich in the afternoon. Return by coach at 8pm back to hotel.
*Friday* to be a rest day, after the match of the previous day.
*Saturday* to travel by train to Toowoomba – then followed by match against Toowoomba and stop at overnight accommodation.
*Sunday* return by train to Brisbane.
*Monday* travel to New South Wales for final leg of Australian tour.

With four matches in eight days including a test match, it was no wonder the tourists were fighting to get a fit side out, all, of course, made worse by long-term injuries. The Lions won all four games. The Brisbane League side was beaten 21–15 in front of 15,722 fans. George Thatcher reported that fans pelted the referee, Mr McKinnon, when he awarded a try to Jack Kitching which clinched the Lions' win. His decision provoked the worst demonstration by supporters for many years. Kitching took a pass 10 yards from the line but a brilliant tackle by Jack Reardon had caused Kitching to stumble, and he lost the ball a yard short of the line.

The tourists had been given little opportunity to rest and almost immediately had to face a powerful Brisbane side that was out to show what their test colleagues had not been able to achieve. Their attitude was that they were more than capable of winning, and would restore lost Australian pride. Another large crowd was in attendance, and the tourists now had to put their faith in their colleagues who had not played in the second test. This faith was more than amply repaid. Willie Davies, the Bradford half-back, had a superb match, revealing the kind of form which would win him the Lance Todd Trophy in 1947. He marshalled the British side superbly and caught the Brisbane defence out of position in the first 10 minutes. He made them pay dearly for this mistake with a beautifully taken individual try. Alfred Drewry praised him, saying: "Davies was the life and soul of the England attack and, in addition to scoring two tries he played a vital part in making two..."

George Curran was proving to be the perfect understudy for Joe Egan, and his constant supply of ball possession from the scrums eased the pressure on the tourists, who led 12–10 at half-time.

In the second half the Australians stepped up the pressure, and throughout most of the half were constantly attacking the British line. Davies once again was able to switch play, and he outwitted the Brisbane defence so completely that he was able to stroll through it. Brisbane were still not to be outdone, however, and immediately upped the stakes. With only 10 minutes to go the scores were level, but once again Davies was equal to the occasion and, with another piece of superb wizardry, he was able to give his club colleague Jack Kitching a huge opening for a try, which was easily converted. Davies was still not finished with his one-man virtuoso performance and finally sealed the victory with an excellent drop-goal. The tourists were fortunate to have such outstanding half-backs in their squad. Davies was an outstanding player who appeared to ooze skills, and had the demeanour of a gentleman.

At this stage of the tour, the newspapers were filled with rumours of the tourists receiving offers from Australian clubs. This reached a crescendo when one newspaper announced that the giant prop, Frank Whitcombe, had already signed for the Sydney club St George. Then it was revealed that a further seven players had received offers, and that Ike Owens was the final one to be offered terms. To read the Australian press one would think that everything was signed, sealed and delivered but, while the Sydney clubs would have sorely liked to have one or more of the tourists in their teams, it became clear that the offers had very little substance, particularly where money was concerned. In the end these offers became something of a joke, with the tourists now asking each other every day which was the latest club to have approached them, and what they would receive.

Surprisingly, a number of the tourists on returning home found offers including their fare to Australia and a cash sum to be paid on arrival, usually around £50. They also learned that they would receive up to £10 per game – this was a decent sum when compared with that of professional footballers who normally received £12 per week.

Despite all the rumours and counter rumours, the tourists still had a job to do: to complete the remaining tour matches undefeated and, most importantly, remain undefeated throughout the test series. They had to get ready almost immediately for another game which would not be easy, against a strong Ipswich team. It was necessary again for several of the tourists to have to play out of position because of injuries, and these included Willie Horne playing at centre and Joe Egan moving into the second row. A number of the side had to play nursing minor injuries. The one bright aspect was that Joe Jones had returned from injury, and was fit to play at full-back. This was a novelty for the tourists, to have a player available for selection who was an actual full-back. It seemed that the position had a jinx on it.

## Ipswich

Two days later, on Thursday 11 July, the Lions beat Ipswich 29–12. The match was made memorable by a superb try scored by Ike Owens just after half-time, leaving the entire Ipswich defence completely demoralised. The ball came loose on the halfway line and Owens wrong footed the defence by not picking the ball up. Like an association footballer, he kicked the ball forward, keeping control of it. Such was Ike's speed that none of his opponents could get near him, let alone attempt to catch him. All the reporters were of the opinion this was the finest ball-and-toe attack, as they described it, and certainly they felt that there was no cause for the Ipswich defence to blame themselves for allowing this score. They added that the move had been so brilliant in concept that it would have opened the most impenetrable defence.

Ipswich had controlled the early play, and at one point actually took the lead. The tourists then turned on their power, especially just before, and after half-time, during which period the match was won. Once again, Willie Davies was in outstanding form and took total control of the play. He went through his full repertoire of wizardry and skills, and this enabled his colleagues to feed off his service. He created a second try for Owens and assisted and dictated many other moves, which led to very simple tries for the scorers. Horne and Lewthwaite both scored a brace of tries, with Knoweldon, Bassett and Egan adding a try each. Only one try was converted, and that was by Willie Horne, not normally noted as a goalkicker, so perhaps the Lions did not suffer too much by having no penalties awarded.

The home team had worn white arm bands as a sign of respect for Les Heidke, whose son had died a few days before the game. He was missed by the Ipswich team. Their other regular prop, Purnell, had to leave the field injured 12 minutes before half time, and went to hospital with a gaping wound in his cheek. Ipswich were a man short for the second half. In 17 games the Lions had scored 495 points, beating the 1932 tourists' record, who had scored 483 in 18 games.

On Saturday 13 July the Lions played Toowoomba. The match programme recalled how the local team had beaten England in 1924. The welcome to the Lions by Keith Jeffries, the Toowoomba Rugby League president, shows how much these matches meant to the local community: "It is with both pride and please that the Toowoomba Rugby League is enabled, after a lapse of 10 years, to offer the hand of good fellowship and extend warmest greetings to members of the touring English team... The visit to Australia of the Englishmen, and their appearance on the playing fields, is an event of supreme importance in the eyes of the sporting community of this country. Firstly, because it affords an opportunity of paying homage to representatives of the Mother Country, and, secondly, to enjoy the exhilarating type of rugby league football the[y] provide. Toowoomba consequently looks upon this Saturday, July 13th, as a gala one in the life of the city... We will greet and cheer them not only for their skill on the field, but as Britishers who battled against almost overwhelming odds to snatch victory right on the final whistle, as it were, in the grim game of war. The majority of our guests saw action in the various Fighting Services, and others toiled tirelessly to back the Fighting Men and Women."

The Lions won 34–5 against the local team. This match saw Trevor Foster's return to action from injury. He was reported to have "played a solid game, indicating that he has at last recovered from the muscle injuries which have kept him out of the greater part of the programme."

This was an eventful match in more ways than one. So many spectators wanted to watch the tourists that every possible viewing position was taken. The crowd was so large that many of the onlookers sought to get a better vantage point by climbing on to the stand roof, although it was not built to carry people. The inevitable happened, and the whole of the roof collapsed, with several hundred spectators on top of it. Before there was any possibility of play, the chaos caused by this occurrence had to be resolved and the debris from the roof cleared.

The start of the match was delayed for more than 30 minutes, a surprisingly short time considering the situation. Several enterprising characters collected carts to use as a grandstand, and charged those who wanted a more elevated view. The other surprising outcome is that amid all the turmoil nobody was seriously injured.

If there were any worries about crowd problems due to people moving forward to follow exciting play, they would have been quickly pacified. Team manager Walter Popplewell had told the players most strongly that they could not afford any more injuries and, as the opposition was hardly likely to be a threat, the Lions were told to slow the game down. The tourists certainly had no intention of playing passing moves at anything like full speed. Nonetheless, the Lions took control of the game straightaway and played it tight without losing possession. They prevented their opponents getting into the game; at times the spectators were so quiet that it was hard to believe there was anyone there.

The biggest cheer of the afternoon was reserved for Fred Hughes, never noted for scoring individual tries, and hardly one of the fastest men in the game, when he scored a solo try. While the tourists may not have made many friends they had a job to do and they followed their manager's directions to the letter.

The scorers in an otherwise uneventful match were White and Batten with two tries apiece, and Kitching, Horne, and Johnson who added one each. Ernest Ward kicked three goals and Risman two. At least the tourists had escaped without any members of the side having sustained a serious injury. This was particularly important, because they had one final match to play four days before the third test, against North Coast, not one of the strongest Australian sides.

The match was on Tuesday 16 July and the Lions won 53–8 in Grafton. Trevor Foster again played, and scored his only try of the tour. Only Whitcombe and Jenkins failed to score. Jim Lewthwaite scored two tries in this game. It was very noticeable that he was a major attraction for young female supporters, and was surrounded by female autograph hunters at the matches, much to his colleagues' amusement. The country games continued to be well attended, with 5,237 in Ipswich, 9,863 in Toowoomba and 6,955 in Grafton.

The standard of refereeing in some matches often left much to be desired. An example of this was in Ipswich, when the British team went through a full match and were never awarded a penalty. This was so unusual that the Australian reporters were sifting through their records to see if this had happened before to a winning side.

## The third test

The issue of the Ashes had been resolved, and the Australian camp felt that its players had not played to their full potential. There were some players who had shown international potential during the season and so the third test was an opportunity to blood them. There was also a feeling that changes were needed, and there were new arrivals from the forces who wished to resume their sporting careers. However, the Australian selectors were probably wise not to make wholesale changes. Most home supporters were sure that the team selected would be good enough to give them a final victory and encouragement for the future of a successful international side.

Ron Bailey withdrew in the week before the match, so Jorgensen took the captaincy again. Edgar Newham was also not selected, and the replacements were both from New South Wales country teams. Boggabri's Trevor Eather took the centre spot, and Kurri Kurri's Noel White played on the wing. For both players the test was their only international appearance for Australia. Clem Kennedy from Souths took over from Grice at scrum-half, and at prop 'Big Jim' Armstrong replaced Westaway. Armstrong played as an amateur because he was a wrestler who went on to represent Australia in the 1948 Olympics. Playing as a professional in rugby league would have disbarred him from the Olympic Games. At loose-forward, Noel Mulligan had recovered from injury and returned to the side.

The tourists were in the familiar position of having to patch up a number of their players. The unfit Frank Whitcombe would be a major loss to the side. However, they were fortunate to have an excellent substitute in George Curran, who was making his Great Britain debut. Although his natural position was hooker, he was also a fine player in the loose, and was very mobile. This is not to disparage Whitcombe who, while a very big man was extremely light on his feet, and had proved extremely dangerous against the Australians, particularly with his sudden darting breaks. There were no doubts about the selection of both Ernest and Ted Ward. They had proved in the last test that both were international-class players and both enhanced the British team. On the wing, Eric Batten replaced Albert Johnson.

The teams were as follows:

*Australia:* Dave Parkinson, Noel White, Joe Jorgenson ( c ), Trevor Eather, Lionel Cooper, Pat Devery, Clem Kennedy, Frank Farrell, George Watt, Jim Armstrong, Arthur Clues, Reg Kay, Noel Mulligan.

*Great Britain:* Ernest Ward, Arthur Bassett, Gus Risman ( c ), Ted Ward, Eric Batten, Willie Horne, Tommy McCue, Ken Gee, Joe Egan, George Curran, Les White, Doug Phillips, Ike Owens.

Referee: Tom McMahon

There was general acceptance that this was currently Australia's best side, although the Queensland press underlined once again that they had been slighted. They were sure that the number of Queensland players should have been increased, particularly after their team's win against the tourists, New South Wales twice failing to beat the Lions.

Another factor raised was that if Australia attempted to take on the British pack in a head-on conflict, then the home side would lose, because the visitors had the skill to keep the game tight even if they lost possession. It was generally agreed that it was up to the home side to keep the game open, and allow their backs to use their speed to really attack the British defence. Interestingly, Arthur Clues says of this period that if the British forwards and Australian backs could have played in the same side it would have been unbeatable.

The Australians hoped that the selection of Mulligan could prevent Owens's surging runs from the scrums. They also felt that he would receive helpful backing from Kennedy. The Australian forwards selected were faster than their predecessors, and it was hoped that their powerful tackling skills would restrain Britain's 'Will o' the Wisp', as Owens was now being called.

The new Australian coach, Rick Johnson, said that the changes should more than cover the previous deficiencies which had occurred in earlier tests, especially around the scrums.

Despite the outcome of the Ashes already having been decided, there was still an extremely good attendance of 35,294 paying at the gates, and approximately 10,000 members attending, who did not appear in the crowd figures. On this occasion there were no problems with the queues at the gates. For the first time the authorities were in control, and there is no mention of any crowd problems. Some of that policing authority could have been very useful later in the game on the pitch, however. All the reporters who covered the match agreed on one thing; without doubt this was one of the most rugged matches ever played in rugby league history.

The Australian forwards had clearly decided that no matter what the press wrote, or thought they were more than capable of taking the Lions forwards in full-pitched battle. They intended to show these so-called 'Indomitables' that they were more than a match for them. Also, it appeared that there were many private scores to settle which had arisen from previous games during the tour. There was certainly not going to be any open play, and the spectators were going to witness a hard, tight, rugged game. The pride of both nations was at stake and, for the Lions, the chance to become the first team to go through an Ashes series unbeaten.

Not for the first time, and certainly not for the last in an international test, two resolute packs were going head to head, with no quarter being asked or given. All the forwards were more than ready to take everything their opponents could throw at them.

This was particularly so in the first half and, despite the Australians being ahead at half-time, the general feeling was that the tourists had won the underlying struggle for control of the game. It would only be a matter of time before they made that supremacy tell.

After only a short period of play in the first half, there was a major affray on the British 25-yard line, with the majority of players on both sides being involved. The referee soon had matters under control and play could continue. Shortly after this display of fisticuffs, the referee then had to read the riot act to both sets of forwards. Les White was chosen to be the referee's sacrificial lamb and, although several other players were equally as involved and just as guilty, so White became the scapegoat and duly received a caution.

The next player to be involved was Ken Gee; he was accused of taking a jab at Arthur Clues. And the backs, for their part, were not to be outdone, with several of them falling foul of the referee. Ted Ward was then involved in successive affrays with Joe Jorgenson and Reg Kay, followed by Eric Batten and George Watt. It was also becoming apparent that the new British selection, George Curran, was involved in a private war with Arthur Clues. Despite all this hostility and bad-tempered behaviour, both sides did have spells of excellent play which was fully appreciated by the crowd. Alfred Drewry commented that "Much of the forward play... was more appropriate to the boxing ring."

After seven minutes, Australian full-back Dave Parkinson had been heavily tackled and injured his leg. He played on, despite being in great pain. It transpired after the game that he had in fact broken it.

For the first time in the series, Australia appeared to have gained more control at the scrums, and as a result their running game was more positive. Even so, one disappointing feature for the home side was that their wingers were starved of the ball, and were rarely involved in the match.

Jorgensen put the home side ahead with a penalty on 17 minutes. Risman missed a kickable penalty, but then kicked a drop-goal from outside the 25 yard line to make the score 2–2. Jorgensen then gave the Australians a 4–2 lead with a 30-yard penalty.

The first try came from Australia and was scored by Clem Kennedy, when he gathered a short kick, ran towards the halfway line and kicked ahead. George Watt picked up the ball, passed as he was tackled to Kennedy who juggled the ball before scoring a great try. Jorgensen missed the kick, and at half-time the home side led 7–2.

**Second half**

In the dressing room at half-time Gus Risman, who was not usually known for making rallying speeches, asked his players to give their all for the last time on the tour, and really show their Australian counterparts what rugby league was really all about.

The tourists' response to this clarion call was immediate, and they took complete control of the game after half-time. They now overwhelmed their opponents, and in six minutes had set up a winning position. First, Risman kicked a penalty. This was immediately followed up by two unconverted tries from Bassett and Curran. The Bassett try was a beauty, cleverly set up by McCue, Owens, Horne and Ernest Ward with Bassett careering down the touch line at full speed, evading White's challenge and scoring in the corner. Curran's try was much a more typical front-rower's effort – following heavy pressure on the home side's line, McCue set him up to use his strength and brawn to touch the ball down. The Lions were 10–7 ahead.

Certainly, sheer frustration can only be the answer to the next misdemeanour, which led to Arthur Clues being sent off. After 63 minutes' play, he struck out at Willie Horne after a tackle and, although his punch missed Horne by a foot, unfortunately for the Australian it was hard to view this as retaliation. The referee was left with little option but to send him off.

Trevor Foster recalls that Clues asked the referee after the match why he had been sent off. His defence was the fact he had missed hitting the British player. The answer he was given, and one an Australian would probably agree with, was because he had missed the Englishman.

With the Australians tiring and now being a man short, the tourists were not in the mood to let them off the hook. Eric Batten set off on a run which left the Australian defenders only clutching at the air when they attempted to tackle him. After tying up half the Australian side, he calmly passed the ball out to where that other speedster Owens was waiting. He was able to cross the line completely unchallenged and used his speed to cut in behind the tryline to make sure that he placed the ball down in a very kickable position. Gus Risman then stepped up and kicked the goal. There was little doubt that the match was as good as over with the Lions 15–7 ahead.

The tourists were not quite finished, however, and began to show all their skills. Following a bout of skilful interpassing, as Ken Gee found an isolated Bassett out on the wing completely unmarked. Bassett must by now have been wondering what the so-called difficulties of scoring in a test match were supposed to be. He also had the extra comfort of choosing where to place the ball after crossing the tryline. Ted Ward was the kicker this time, and was given the opportunity of being able to successfully complete the scoring, making the final result 20–7.

The Lions were comfortable winners in the end. Risman who had led his troops with so much calmness and diplomacy, became the worthy first recipient of the Claude Corbett Memorial Trophy which is now always awarded to the winning captain of an Ashes series. Claude Corbett was at one time arguably Australia's most famous rugby league reporter and was the only newspaperman to receive life membership of the New South Wales Rugby League. He died of cancer in 1944, and his brother had donated the award in his memory. It was a fitting award for Risman, whose service to the Lions as a tourist went back to 1932. The third test had marked his final test appearance, because he did not play against New Zealand.

Harry Sunderland said that Risman had "carried the responsibilities of leadership with a graceful calm... as great a figure as has ever been touted, whether on the playing field or at the banquet table when making most concise, well-phrased and diplomatic speeches."

Presentation of the Ashes to Walter Popplewell at Tattersall's Club. (DP)

Programmes from the second and third tests.
(Courtesy Mike Inman & Peter Lush)

The referee, Tom McMahon, commented after the game: "I give full credit of England's 20–7 win in [the] rugby league test to their captain, Gus Risman. You had to be out in the middle to realise the inspiration Risman was to the players, and how he drove them to victory. When England took the field in the second half, trailing 7–2, Risman said: 'Now, boys, you have to save this game for England, let them have it.' His men replied by scoring eight points in six minutes, clinching the game for England. After each score, Risman said: 'Come on boys; more of that.' He also sympathised when his players made a mistake. There was none of that with the Australian side, who just took things as they came. Although the England team are not as good as their 1936 combination, the present side were far too good for Australia in all departments of the game."

After the match, the Australian press was filled with comments from the Australian players, who related how dirty and undisciplined the game had been, and how the referee had allowed it to develop. Also, their tales were full of remarks about how they had suffered innumerable illegal challenges, and the referee had allowed play to go on outside the rules of the game. These reports made the oft-repeated Australian criticism of whinging Poms look rather hypocritical, and certainly did little credit to the individuals involved. The only British tourist who made any remark about the rough play during the game was the indefatigable prop Ken Gee, who briefly commented that "we expect test matches to be tough, otherwise why play them?"

However, Ian Heads and David Middleton in their centenary history of rugby league in Australia quote Harry Sunderland as saying after the game: "There was more downright bad sportsmanship and disgusting bad temper than I have seen in 36 years of watching rugby league."

Reflecting on the tour, Gus Risman said that "It has been a very happy tour, and we have received wonderful hospitality wherever we have gone. I must pay tribute to England's wonderful forwards who, facing adversity caused by injuries, did not complain of overwork." He added that "Our opponents gave their all, and played with true Australian tenacity to make this a hard-fought series."

Despite their claims about the Lions, the Australian players were criticised. Former international forward Frank Burge said that the forwards were "cream puffs" compared to their predecessors, although this may have been a veteran player remembering his own playing days through rose-tinted spectacles. The ARL president Jersey Flegg said that both teams were below their pre-war standards. This view was supported by Wilf Gabbatt, who said that "I had many confidential talks with members of the Australian Board of Control, and New South Wales and Queensland Leagues, and I found a sincere desire at the earliest possible moment to attain the pre-war standard of football."

Gus Risman caused some controversy, saying to J.C. Graham of the *Daily Dispatch*: "Compared with the standards revealed in my two previous tours, play in Australia has deteriorated 50 per cent. When the Australians found they couldn't outplay us in the tests they tried rough tactics. These methods were a great mistake, for you cannot produce good play by these means." In 1994, Trevor Foster reflected that "There was some nasty business. It was kill or be killed. The Australians would try anything to beat us and you had to stand your corner. If you didn't, they would take full advantage."

Although the Lions had been clear winners on the scoreboard, Alan Whiticker and Ian Collis say that "the closeness" of the game "was not reflected on the scoreboard". Robert Gate says that the Lions victory "was overwhelmingly flattering to their efforts and scant justice to those of the Australians."

Right to the very end of the Australian tour the tourists maintained their calm demeanour, and to their credit were prepared to manage anything fate could throw at them. So much during the tour had gone wrong for them, including the depressing number of injuries to players in key positions, which had often caused many of the tourists to have to play matches out of their usual position; in addition to the onerous travelling schedules they faced.

Travelling arrangements all along had been far from perfect, with numerous hold-ups, and too often the players had to travel vast distances prior to important games.

The third test match was the last game for the tourists on Australian soil. The final leg of the tour was to be in New Zealand, with just one test match to play alongside six other matches. The Lions were soon to make history by becoming the first sporting touring side to fly from one country to another. The tour management's change of heart surrounding flying had been a morale booster to the tourists, and arrangements for departure to New Zealand were made at a cost of £30 per player.

The tourists now knew that they had become the first British touring test team to be unbeaten in a three-test Australian series. This record stands today, and given the recent history of matches against the Australians and the current structure of tours and the international set up of the game, is unlikely to be beaten in the foreseeable future.

Trevor Foster and Joe Jones with a reporter in Brisbane
(Courtesy Simon Foster)

Great Britain versus North Coast at Grafton on 16 July 1946.
(Courtesy Simon Foster)

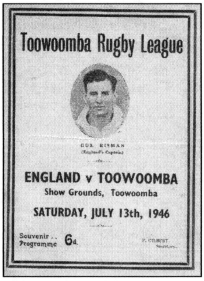

Programmes from the second half of the tour in Australia.
(All courtesy Mike Inman except Toowoomba, courtesy Peter Lush)

# 9. New Zealand

Plans had now been completed for the New Zealand part of the tour which would comprise of seven matches. However, the major problem had been how to get the tourists across the Tasman Sea, because there were no definite sailings at that time.

The two managers took the momentous decision to fly the party to New Zealand. They travelled on flying boat aircraft. The party would have to be split into three groups as the planes available on this service did not have enough passenger accommodation for everyone. The heavy luggage had to go by sea, and would arrive around four weeks later. The first flight was on 21 July and took eight hours. It included Eddie Waring who had newspaper and broadcasting commitments. The second and third flights were on the next two days. Much has been made of this first flight by a touring team, and the fact that it took three flights. The myth has grown up that it was because of the danger of flying, and of course the tragic accident suffered by the Manchester United side in Munich in 1958 have probably increased that idea. The answer is quite simple, that passenger aircraft able to carry large numbers of passengers were simply not available.

Already the tourists had been away from home almost four months, and considerably longer for those who had been serving in the armed forces right up until the last moment of the voyage from Britain. On arrival in New Zealand the tourists were met by a spell of warm dry weather. They were lodged in a hotel in Auckland, which was much better than any accommodation they had encountered in Australia.

There had been uncertainty over the New Zealand leg of the tour because the Lions' management had to be sure of being able to book places on a ship to return to England. Wilf Gabbatt wrote in the tour report: "Previous to our departure from Australia the New Zealand League were somewhat perturbed by our not readily agreeing to visit New Zealand. I assured them that we had every intention of fulfilling our obligations but until we had an assurance that our return passage to England had been arrange, I could not agree to tour New Zealand."

After the media pressures in Australia, the tourists were to find that life was quieter in New Zealand. But that is possibly because following the war, rugby league in New Zealand was struggling. Some Auckland clubs had amalgamated to survive, and playing numbers were well down in Canterbury. In Wellington they had been particularly hard hit by military mobilisation. The game there was only just surviving, and to make matters worse it was a rugby union stronghold from whom they also faced prejudice. West Coast and Waikato had stayed strong because of the coal miners, who were exempt from military service.

A fraught inter-code wrangle took place in Christchurch about the match against South Island on Saturday 27 July. On 15 June Alfred Drewry reported that "The tourists will not be allowed to play on Lancaster Park, the best Christchurch ground, when they visit New Zealand... This ground is controlled by the rugby union. The decision caused a controversy in New Zealand, most people considering that the relegation of a match by the Englishmen to a second class ground is a slight."

The dispute escalated when the rugby union authorities provocatively arranged a counter attraction between the New Zealand Army touring team and Canterbury. The issue was debated in Parliament and by the Christchurch City Council. Despite widespread anger over rugby union's stance, the only concessions were to allow the tourists the use of Addington Show grounds, and to alter their kick-off time to avoid a direct clash.

The Canterbury mayor, E.H. Andrews, showed where his sympathies lay by ceremonially kicking off the league game. The Lions won 24–12. The South Island team was dominated by West Coast players. Two brothers scored tries for South Island, centre Bill Mountford and his brother, Ken, their loose-forward. Their brother Ces was ready to sail the following week to take up a three-year contract with Wigan. He went on to complete a career record of 76 tries and 57 goals, becoming one of New Zealand rugby league's icons. For the tourists, Jim Lewthwaite – although he did not play in a test on this tour – kept up a remarkable scoring performance by adding a hat trick of tries. However, conditions were different from Australia, and the forwards would have to adapt to muddy pitches in New Zealand.

Former new Zealand Rugby League Council member Bud Lisle recalls attending the match as a school student: "The Kiwi Army side came to watch the Lions match. They had played in the morning. They came to watch England as they had fought together in the war, and wanted to watch the tourists. They didn't want their game to clash. They were standing in front of me in uniform."

The touring party had a number of players who were carrying injuries from the Australian part of the tour, and it was decided that Martin Ryan, Jack Kitching, Dai Jenkins and Harry Murphy would probably not be fit to participate on this leg of the tour.

The weather also changed with the move to New Zealand and there were continuous days of heavy rain. The tourists sailed by boat to Greymouth under dark skies to play West Coast on Monday 29 July.

Eddie Waring had been upset about the bad feeling between the rugby league game and union authorities, and sought to try and bring the two sides together. On the ship to play West Coast was the New Zealand Army rugby union side. Some of them had played in the post-war victory internationals in Britain, and knew a number of the Lions. Ike Owens had played for the British rugby union team in that series.

In the latter part of the war two matches featuring rugby league teams playing their union counterparts had taken place. These were forces personnel and played under union rules – with the League XV winning both times. Waring in a letter to the New Zealand Rugby Union ruling body suggested a joint match with proceeds of the game going to purchase food for Britain.

Sadly, he never received any response. Indeed, the hostility of the New Zealand union authorities to rugby league saw them inform Ilkley Rugby Union Club that they must not allow the 1947–48 New Zealand Kiwis to train on their ground, after they had said they were willing for their facilities to be used.

In the short period prior to the game there had not been enough time for the opposing parties to discuss the referee's interpretations of the rules. In this match the Lions definitely regretted this, as they would for the rest of the tour, and a fine game by Gus Risman, including two tries, could not help prevent the largest defeat of the tour, 17–8.

After Ken Mountford had scored a third try in the 55th minute, West Coast never looked like losing. The tourists got 23 penalties, but conceded 26. Nothing though can take credit away from their opponents' outstanding tackling carried out by both backs and forwards which completely threw the tourists. Doug Phillips wrote that "The ground was very muddy from one end to the other." It was the first defeat for the Lions in New Zealand since 1928.

The rumours about players being recruited by Australian clubs continued. The latest target was Harry Murphy, who despite being injured for most of the tour, had apparently been offered £300 by Balmain, £9 a match and an end of season bonus. He did not sign and continued his career with Wakefield.

The tourists were involved in their third match in five days on Wednesday 31 July against a Maori representative side in Wellington. The Lions were introduced to the New Zealand Governor-General, Sir Bernard Freyberg, before the match.

Trevor Foster may have felt he had been kicking his heels in Australia due to injury, but had yet to miss a match in New Zealand. Once again the Lions incurred the wrath of the referee and this time had an astonishing 22–0 penalty deficit. Yet the tourists treated the game as an exhibition match, and threw the ball about at every opportunity. This was helped by opponents who were somewhat hesitant in the tackle – the final result was a convincing 32–8 win. The majority of the press rated the tourists' performance of all-round rugby skills as the best of the whole tour. There was a match award for the most outstanding player which was won by Bryn Knowelden, and certainly put him in the frame for selection for the forthcoming test against New Zealand. Alfred Drewry said that "Few combinations could have stood up to Ernest Ward's men today". On the refereeing, he said that the standard "is as poor as it was in Australia with few exceptions" and he said there was some justification for the players cynically calling them "one eyed".

However, on this occasion the opposition had allowed the tourists' performance to be somewhat overrated. In their history of Maori rugby league, John Coffey and Bernie Wood say that "...the Maori had very little time to prepare for the match and their experience was not enough to counter the British professionals, who were determined to regain their winning ways. The Lions also appreciated the ideal conditions, the firm Basin Reserve playing surface contrasting with the muddy grounds they had struck down south." However, the *Auckland Star* correspondent described the Maori tackling as "very half-hearted".

The long train journey back to Auckland was enlivened by members of the Maori team, who were travelling with the Great Britain party. The Maoris taught Fred Hughes, Eric Batten, Trevor Foster, Ernest Ward and some other tourists a Maori war dance. Then the Lions tried unsuccessfully to teach the Maoris how to sing *Ilkley Moor Bah' t 'at*.

On Thursday 8 August, the tourists were invited as guests to Parliament House, where the Prime Minister, Peter Fraser, who had been born in Scotland, and other members of the New Zealand Parliament, made them very welcome.

The continuous wet weather was affecting everyone, but it made little impact on team selection. Both tour managers caught heavy colds, but the players managed to remain healthy.

Three of the four final matches of the tour were played at Carlaw Park, Auckland. The game against Auckland, despite the most atrocious conditions attracted a crowd reported as 15,000 or 20,000, and was notable for the hundreds of seagulls on the areas of the field where there was no play.

The conditions were so awful that there was no chance of any open play. The tourists scored three tries to their opponents' one, although Auckland also kicked two penalties. Even though the Lions deserved their 9–7 win, it required a superb covering tackle by Eric Batten to prevent his opposing winger from scoring a late try which would have won the match. Once again the tourists had suffered on the penalty count, although the tally on this occasion was somewhat reduced at 16–6. Doug Phillips wrote that "It was the biggest mudbath I'd ever seen. Had a job to distinguish our boys from the opponents." Alfred Drewry commented that the conditions were "farcical" and that they had been made worse by the preliminary games on the pitch. The players were so muddy that Risman tackled Nicholson by mistake, having thought he was an Auckland player.

The next game was at Huntley. Despite the continuing wet weather the side played an enjoyable match against South Auckland.

Doug Phillips chases a loose ball against West Coast at Greymouth. (DP)

The tourists were received by Princess De Peau at Huntley, and watched a display of Maori dancing. (DP)

Dai Jenkins was back to match fitness, and played alongside fellow scrum-half Tommy McCue. These two players were the only ones who had yet to score points on tour. The Lions treated the game as an exhibition by throwing the ball about and tried to give Jenkins and McCue the opportunity to finally score. Late on in the second half, Dai Jenkins dummied the opposing full-back to score behind the posts, and the South Auckland spectators found it hard to understand the particularly vociferous applause from the tourists for his effort.

Unfortunately, McCue was unable to copy his team mate, and was to complete the tour scoreless, but nothing could take away the outstanding reputation he had gained as the world's greatest scrum-half. Albert Johnson had a match to remember, scoring a hat-trick of tries. But there was a downside to this match, which had been enjoyed by the tourists, and that was Gus Risman's terrible performance at full-back. He experienced all sorts of handling problems, and afterwards decided not to take part in what would most probably have been his final international match. To add to the woes, hooker Joe Egan sustained a serious knock which prevented him playing in the last two games of the tour.

Three days later, on Saturday 10 August, the tourists were back at Carlow Park to face New Zealand in the only test played on this leg of the tour. Test debuts were given to Joey Jones, Bryn Knowelden and Trevor Foster, who was aged 31. Sadly, no place could be found for Jim Lewthwaite, the tour's leading scorer, but in his case time seemed to be on his side, although actually he never won a Great Britain cap.

It was also a time of change for the New Zealanders who included three players who had been on the 1939 tour to Great Britain that was cut short by the outbreak of war. These were wingers Roy Nurse and Bill Mountford, who were to make their only test appearance, along with prop Bruce Graham. All three were not selected for the forthcoming 1947–48 tour of Great Britain and France.

The sides were as follows:

*New Zealand:* Warwick Clarke, Roy Nurse, Len Jordan, Maurie Robertson, Bill Mountford, Roy Clark, Rex Cunningham, John Newton, Bob Aynsley, Bruce Graham, Arthur Gillman, Charlie McBride, Travers Hardwick.
*Great Britain:* Joe Jones, Eric Batten, Ernest Ward, Bryn Knowelden, Albert Johnson, Willie Davies, Tommy McCue, Bob Nicholson, George Curran, Ken Gee, Les White, Trevor Foster, Ike Owens.
*Referee:* J. Donovan

Thankfully the match started in dry weather, although the playing area was saturated. The first half was a tight affair with once again the home country seemingly favoured as the tourists fell foul of the referee on his interpretation of play-the-ball.

Open play was almost nonexistent and the game was being spoilt for both players and spectators by the continuous blowing of the

102

referee's whistle. The New Zealanders took a 6–0 lead, through three penalties kicked by Warwick Clarke, a very reliable goalkicker.

At half-time, the heavens once more opened and the remainder of play took place in continuous rain. The second half began with much more assertive play from the tourists, and it was not long before Batten broke clear and scored, but his try was not converted. Ernest Ward then made his mark on the match by scoring a try, and shortly afterwards kicked a penalty to put the Lions 8–6 ahead. New Zealand were on the back foot, but then a stroke of luck affected the result.

Warwick Clarke was taking a penalty kick from close to the touchline, and his effort struck an upright and rebounded into play. Bruce Graham may have been making his debut for New Zealand but he was alert, caught the rebound, and made an unstoppable charge beneath the posts. Clarke's simple conversion put the Kiwis 11–8 ahead, and a further goal from Clarke completed the scoring.

The general view was that although luck may have played a part, the Kiwis deserved to win through, due to the fact that their forwards had the better of the scrums and in the loose. Determined tackling by the home backs also negated much of the Lions' advantage in speed and backline skills. Doug Phillips reflected that "We played the wrong type of game. Did not suit the weather or field."

After the game Tommy McCue spoke very strongly about the play-the-ball requirements of the New Zealand referee, but Eddie Waring was probably correct in stating that the need to achieve international agreement on the rules required the formation of an international body for rugby league.

Two days later an extra match was played on the same ground against Auckland. Everyone's attention was on Ernest Ward who was the tourists' leading points scorer with 91, and whether he could attain a century. There was surprise at the start of the game when Gus Risman captained the side for his last match as a tourist, because most people thought he had been unfit for the test, which was not the case. Reports indicate that Gus gave a faultless display, and showed everyone what an outstanding player he was. Ernest Ward was in brilliant form and kicked five goals, the last of which was a fine touchline conversion of a Jim Lewthwaite try. The referee blew his whistle for time after the ball sailed between the posts, and Ernest achieved his unique feat on the very last play of the tour.

Once again problems with the referee and interpretations of the law affected the tourists. They were so incensed with his interpretation of play-the-ball in the first half that they threatened not to play the second half unless something was said to the referee. New Zealand officials intervened and his decisions were more acceptable to the tourists in the second half. They had been penalised 15 times in the first half.

After such a long period away from home and due to the various discomforts they had been required to undergo, the players all signed and submitted a letter to the Rugby League Council, which they handed to Wilf Gabbatt on Thursday 8 August, shortly before their departure from New Zealand. The letter read as follows: "The Council is well aware that, during this tour, considerable inconvenience has been caused to the whole party in travel and accommodation which would not normally have been incurred, involving everyone in extra expenses which have had to be met out of their own pockets. Clothes have been ruined and in some cases lost. The success of the tour, both financially and otherwise, was due in no small measure to the way the players stood up to this gruelling without complaint and we feel that we are entitled to some measure of compensation."

There was no doubt that the players were put in an invidious situation due to the length of the tour and the fact that in their ever-changing travel arrangements many of the players had lost articles of clothing, and all too often personal items had been ruined. Unfortunately, the Lions' plea fell on deaf ears, in that the Rugby League Council decided that the tour bonus of £123 per player was quite sufficient.

As the players were leaving New Zealand, there was yet another report about a tourist being recruited by an Australian club. The Canterbury Bankstown secretary claimed that an England player, believed to be Martin Ryan, had asked for £1,000 to sign, and another wanted £500. Both also wanted jobs and homes. Once again, no one actually moved to Australia.

On 14 August the return home began with the party's departure from Wellington aboard the passenger liner HMS Rangitiki which, by a strange coincidence, was the same ship which had brought the ill-destined New Zealand rugby league party to Britain in 1939. They were due to make a three-week crossing of the Pacific Ocean to Panama, because the Rangitiki was taking a party of GI brides to New York. These were young girls who had become engaged or married to American servicemen.

The early part of the voyage was generally in good sailing conditions. However on 4 September the ship was hit by lightening in a storm, which caused a small fire.

Not surprisingly the GI brides showed great consternation when after passing through the Panama Canal they were diverted to Halifax, Nova Scotia because of a dock strike at New York. After the prospective brides had been disembarked, the ship sailed from Halifax on 14 September.

Before the party had realised they could not stop in New York, there had been consideration of playing a match there. Wilf Gabbatt says that a meeting was arranged with the captain, including both tour

The RMS Rangitiki in the Panama Canal. (DP)

managers, Walter Crockford and members of the press. The captain was asked if a match, in his opinion, could be played. Wilf Gabbatt wrote that "I interjected at this point... was no concern of his. Looking back at the sequence of events, I am of the opinion that this project had been previously discussed with the captain." Again, reading between the lines, all was not well between the tour managers. As there was no rugby league in New York, presumably it would have been an exhibition match of two teams selected from the tourists.

Much of the final leg of the trip was quite rough, and they docked at Tilbury on 22 September at 10pm, four days late. The party had been away from home for nearly six months, and some of the party had still to get clearance from the armed forces. They were met at Tilbury by the RFL secretary, and the chairman of the Rugby League Council W.H. Hughes and three other Council members Bob Anderton, Richard Lockwood and Harry Hornby. Ike Owens gathered his Welsh Choir together, and they gave a final rendering of *Sospan Fach* the Llanelli Welsh rugby song, which had been very popular in Australia.

Some of the players' families were completely unaware that their loved ones were home. Trevor Foster recalled that on his return to the family home in Newport, his mother was at the cinema, and a message was flashed on the screen to let her know he was home.

Unfortunately, many players on their arrival home found that the food parcels they had sent from Australia had failed to arrive, but this disappointment was soon forgotten at the joy of finally being home with their loved ones, and to once again embark on a civilian life.

*****

Mike Gardner describes in his biography of Willie Horne how the Barrow players and Wilf Gabbatt arrived at Barrow Central Station on Monday 24 September at 10.25pm, to be met by the deputy mayor and a large crowd of supporters. Barrow had made a poor start to the

105

season, because they were deprived of four of their key players, who had been on tour. But the next Saturday they were back in action, playing against Rochdale Hornets.

No doubt the other players underwent similar experiences, being welcomed home, returning to work and picking up the game again with their clubs.

Probably at that time they did not realise the size of their achievement. They had played a major part in re-establishing international rugby league after the greatest war that mankind had ever endured. The future tours, and clashes between Great Britain, Australia and New Zealand owed so much to the Indomitables.

# Doug Phillips's tour diary

**Publishers' note:** We would like to thank Sherill, the daughter of
Doug Phillips, and Simon Foster for the opportunity to include this diary
in the book. We have edited it to take out some personal information,
mainly about letters and presents, and occasionally where we could
not read Doug's writing. Any gaps are indicated by … . Any additions
by us are shown [ ]. We hope readers find it of interest.

### Tuesday 2 April
Left home on the 6.20am bus, caught the 7.07am train. Picked up Ike Owens
at Bridgend. Changed at Bristol, picked up Trevor Foster. Arrived at Plymouth
(North Road station) 2.30pm. Waited for arrival of team from London at
3.15pm. Waited for arrival of team from London, at 3.15pm, then proceeded
to HMS Indomitable.

After getting our kit on board we had a cup of tea, bread, butter & jam.
Afterwards we got our cabins, and shared with Fred Hughes and Les White.

Had a lot of photos taken on and off the ship. Had dinner at 7.30pm after
which Ike Owens, Fred Hughes and myself went into Plymouth and had a few
drinks before returning. Got in about 10.30pm.

I wrote a couple of letters [home]. I received a telegram from Ronnie and
that ended the day.

### Wednesday 3 April
Got called at 7am but didn't get up till just 8 and were last joining for
breakfast, but were on time. Got a lot of photos taken again on the flight deck,
met Bob Sloman (ex Oldham player). Had a photo taken speaking to him by
*Daily Mail*. Got a paper with our photo in it of arrival at the station the day
previous.

The same three of us went out to town for lunch and again met Bob
Sloman. He took us in his car to his hotel, called the Friendship. It was a
beautiful place, and well located, on top of the hill overlooking the town.

Got a taxi back by 2.30pm and met another (ex Oldham player) by the
name of Wise, played 1910 to 1915. Wrote to Ronnie and got a letter from his
father when I got here. The weather was simply scorching.

The ship pulled out at 5.30pm. We had a cup of tea before this and again
had dinner at 7.30pm.

After sitting down relaxing for a while, I retired to my cabin went for a
bath and am now in bed writing. So the day is finished, also my writing.

### Thursday 4 April
Got called at 7, got up at 10 past and went for breakfast. The food up to now
is very good, no complaints. After breakfast we strolled the flight deck and got
our blazer and flannels at 10, also one towel.

The ship is sailing quite well. But up to now I'm feeling pretty good. We're
somewhere in the Bay of Biscay and our speed is about 18 knots.

We three went to the canteen, bought two pennants (inscribed the HMS
Indomitable) also 2 pairs of socks (black) and 2 bars of chocolate. After that
we managed to get a cup of tea from the ratings and returned to our mess

room (warrant officers). There they gave us the rules of the mess and asked us to co-operate. Then followed lunch, which again was exceptionally food, everyone enjoyed it, and am now in bed for 40 winks.

We have been asked to wear our blazers on board, to distinguish us from a few other civvies.

Got up from bed at 4pm, went for a cup of tea, went up on flight deck, returned, played draughts, then had dinner, after which we returned to the cabin. I wrote three letters, one to the Supporters Club, one to Mr Travis to thanks them for their gifts of £5/5/0 and £1. Wrote to Mr Cocker. But had to give up – the ship was beginning to roll. So I got to bed, it was 10pm.

## Friday 5 April

Forgot to put my watch back one hour. But got called at the correct time and was having breakfast at ¼ past 8. Sat down till 9am when we all had to go to the Aft deck where we all met the Captain and had a few more photos taken. We also had a few taken immediately after on the flight deck.

Went in search of a cup of tea and succeeded. Returned to the flight deck for a while till 11.30, when we went and got paid (our first pay day). £1/10/0. Sat down till lunch and am here in the cabin doing a bit of letter writing [home] and Oldham RFC.

Spent the rest of the afternoon on the flight deck in the sun, watching various Navy teams play deck hockey.

Tea at 4pm. Bought another pennant, changed clothes with a Navy Warrant Officer along with Tommy McCue and went for dinner. It was good laugh, and had genuine phone call and I tried to bluff him on, but found out it wasn't a joke. We ended up with a good sing song. We tried to get our photos taken, but couldn't find Waring until it went too dark.

The sing song finished at 10pm. Got my clothes changed again and into bed.

## Saturday 6 April

Got called at 6am by one of the boys for the ship was entering Gibraltar. I got up at 10 past 6. Washed and went up on the flight deck, the ship came to a stop. So as nothing was happening Fred and myself went for a cup of tea which we got at our mess. But had to wait for breakfast.

After breakfast we had a shave and saw a lot of small boats pull towards the ship selling watches and cloths. I got a big tablecloth, all ... for £2. Fred bought one earlier for £2/10/0. The watches were all prices.

Passed some of our time on the flight deck watching the traffic and a few times the hose pipe was switched on to them to drive them away.

Played deck hockey ... just after the ship pulled out of the harbour after it had finished refuelling. We drew 2–2. Had a bit of tea and away for dinner at 9.00pm. We went to a cinema show in the lower hangar, saw *Shine on Harvest Moon*, quite good.

Had our first Saturday night toast to the folks at home after dinner. Out of pictures at 11 and so to bed.

Eddie Waring (news reporter) went ashore. Bought back four lovely watches worth £100 in England, if not more. He bought back a package of oranges and shared them around.

## Sunday 7 April

Felt very tired, after being called at 7am. Stopped in bed until 20 to 8 and it was late getting to breakfast. We were the last. Didn't go on church parade. But went back to cabin laid and read till lunch time.

After lunch I did a bit of washing then laid reading for the rest of the time till tea. Played draughts with Willie Davies, then went back to the cabin to read till dinnertime.

Went to the pictures and saw Abbot and Costello in *The Society*. Had seen it before but it passed the time off.

Very high keen wind (head on). Ship was twisted half around, the sea is very choppy but the ship is ploughing through it a treat. Don't fell it rocking at all.

## Monday 8 April

Clocks got put on one hour in the early hours of morning. But forgot mine till getting up when I was told. So it was then 8am. Made a rush for breakfast, then shaved afterwards.

Had a meeting at 11am. But not of great importance. It was just follow common sense. A day of writing now, for all mail has to be in by 10 tonight so that they can be posted at Malta in the morning after docking there for putting passengers off.

Put name down for a photo of the ship. Also saw a snap with one of the players (Bryn Knowelden) which he took on the flight deck before leaving Plymouth, with Ike, Fred, Harry Sunderland and Bob Sloman. Wrote letters [home]. Got the photo of the ship that I'd already ordered.

Had dinner then an early night after washing my sports shirt, pairs of socks, then put my point shirt to soak. Put my watch forward half hour. Played deck hockey and drew again 3–3. I managed to score one from halfway. But it was luck.

PS Got told at the meeting they're trying to get us back via New York and Canada to Liverpool.

## Tuesday 9 April

The time now is 2 hours in advance of British time. Got into Malta about 8.15am while having breakfast. Went into Malta about 10.30. Had a good stroll around, had a lovely dinner, egg, chop and chips, with bread and a drink, and had lovely ice-cream afterwards.

Walked around for a while again then went to the pictures as life a bit quiet during the afternoon.

Came out, had another meal of double egg and chips, then went looking for presents (souvenirs). Bought two little handkerchiefs, then a 'duchess et'.

Strolled round the pubs, having a singsong, finding out what life was like. It was deadly.

Had supper after of pork steak and chips, tea and bread & butter. So it was a real day of eating. I enjoyed it, got back on board about ¼ to 11pm. Met a chap from Oldham, Robinson of Brook St.

## Wednesday 10 April

Left Malta at 8.30am while having breakfast, walked along the flight deck for some time. Fixed up two netball stands and nets in one of the hangars, 5 of us had a run about. But it was hot for us ... and did we perspire, we were soaking.

Had a good rub down. Then washed out my print shirt, have a slight headache. But a lay down will cool that.

After tea watched a few of the boys play hockey, they lost 5–1. Had a bath after then dinner. After dinner went to the pictures. Saw Noel Coward's *Brief Encounter,* but the poor talking spoiled it. Got out just before the finish and so to bed.

### Thursday 11 April
Lovely weather, just a nice breeze. Played basketball for ... 40 minutes. But it was too much of the all-in stuff. Had a lovely bath. Then nice cold lunch. Sort of salad and cold meat. Wrote [letters].

Sent a parcel home ... Went to picture saw (*Two Yards Abroad*). Quite a good show.

### Friday 12 April
Got up at 8am for I went to sleep after being called. Got shaved after breakfast then put on a pair of shorts and kept in them till 6.30pm, except for lunch when I put my greys and shirt on for the meal.

Arrived at Port Said approx. 8.30am. Entered the Suez Canal about 10am and about 25 to 8pm we anchored in a place called Bitter Lakes for the night.

We passed through El Ballah and near to ... . Passed various camps which were situated alongside the Suez. The houses or huts the actual inhabitants lived in were worse than the tents I used to build while a youngster from old mats and tin sheets. It didn't seem possible for people to live in them.

We passed the aircraft carrier The Queen at 11.30am in the canal, but didn't pass any others except the crafts of the inhabitants, sand weird looking things they were. Got paid at 11.30 and got my expenses as well for when I travelled to Plymouth to start with. So I got in all £4/0/0 (£2/10/0 expenses).

Made out a list of things I want from the shops and handed it in to Gus Risman. Hope we'll get all. I'm sorry I didn't ask for pyjamas as the ones I bought will undoubtedly shrink after washing ... Turning in early tonight at 9pm, but writing in bed. Saw memorial for Aussies and New Zealanders of 1914-18. Wrote to Mam.

### Saturday 13 April
Played a game of basketball during the morning. But sat down on a gun turret reading and singing up till the game at 10.30am. Anchored last night at Bitter Lakes got on the move early in the morning when anchored approx 8.20am for they wanted to finish painting the side of the ship. We stopped just after leaving the Canal. In the Suez Canal Bay but only for 2 hours then proceeded to the Red Sea. The weather was very warm and a warm breeze.

Before dinner, 3.30pm, played deck-hockey and got a bang on the lip, but it a little, and loosened two of my teeth, I might have to get them out. Wrote [letters]. Played Tombola after dinner 9.15pm, Fred won one game. Then we were 6d in pocket, for we shared the profits.

Passed the spot where the picture *Four Feathers* was acted.

110

**Sunday 14 April**

Another warm day but had a slight breeze in it. Had a photo of the team taken at 9.30am, and didn't go near the flight deck after that till 2.30pm.Stayed for an hour.

Put the clocks forward another half hour, making 2½ hours before home time. Did a bit of washing and also ironed two shirts which I'd washed a few days ago. Wrote [letters]. Is very stuffy in the cabin room 11.15pm. Have just come from the picture show *Spanish Main*. Had seen it before in London. Going to sleep on top of the bed tonight.

**Monday 15 April**

Put clocks on half hour this morning again, making it 3 hours in advance of home time, a very warm day again, but not what one could call bright sunshine. It was up strong, then as if it was clouded out.

Got these articles of kit from the stores: 2 tropical shirts, 2 pairs of white socks, 2 pairs sandals and half dozen handkerchiefs for £1/9/2. Watch one of our teams play in the knock out competition of deck-hockey. They won 4–1. Went to pictures saw *The Last Chance*.

A very strong wind blew up just before the hockey match and the sea quite choppy and it still is. The ship is only rolling slightly. Fred and Les have their beds up on deck. So I'm on my own tonight. Wrote letters [home].

**Tuesday 16 April**

Arrived in Aden at 9.15am. Spent the morning walking about. Had a bath, then dressed up in our whites for lunch and got our photos taken. 'The Three' on the Flight Deck by Bryn Knowelden, then went ashore.

Arrived in harbour at 1.30pm. Walked around for a while (called Waterhead). But the conditions of people were disgusting, and very filthy people and houses and shacks.

Were lucky Ike and myself bought two net shirts, 5/3 each. Went into Aden itself, that was just as bad. So returned at 6.20pm to the ship. Saw Crown Prince of the Yemeni place arrive, had to have a shower when I got back, felt itchy. Had a good singsong until Dai Jenkins spoilt it. Tasted water melon. Wrote [home].

**Wednesday 17 April**

Started raining, but didn't do much, just a heavy shower, just damped the place down. Still warm and clammy in the cabin, but nice and breezy up on the flight deck. Left Aden at 10.15am. Had a walk around the deck. Had a large portion of water melon given us. And we also had a piece after dining tonight. They were the gift of the Crown Prince of Yemen after his visit yesterday. Played hockey in the 1st squad ands won 7–0. Our other team, known as Wigan Wallopers won 1–0, so our four teams are the seconds round and stand a fairly good chance.

We've got to move out of our present warrant officers' mess, but will get full particulars in the morning. Am in the cabin on my own again tonight. The other two sleeping on deck. But I don't relish putting my palisade on the deck for my clothes would get all messed up as that part isn't very clean.

Clocks on an hour tonight again, making it 4 hours ahead of home time. Am starting writing [home] and will keep doing a bit till we reach Colombo.

### Thursday 18 April

Was still warm and close in the cabin. But have had the fan put right again, and it's running alright now, and makes a vast difference to us in there.

The Tourist Terrors played in the second round, and lost 4–2. First half they were the best, but lacked positioning. Had a lovely bath and shower, a lay down and off to dinner. I was in bed again before 9pm, for I had a slight headache. But I couldn't sleep for hours. It was a bit stuffy but I kept thinking of everything in general, which in turn kept me awake.

Past the island of Socotra off Somali, which is at the bottom of Abyssinia. Putting the clock on tonight again. 4½ hours ahead.

### Friday 19 April (Good Friday)

Went to a church service on the quarter deck, and the signing was alright. I enjoyed it. But the captain reading out the service was pretty poor.

We've moved to a mess of our won. Started with lunch there. Have drawn a camp bed and have pout it on deck, and I intend sleeping there tonight. Slept on deck after put clocks on ½ hour again, making it 5 hours. Wrote [home]. Had Swinton in the sweep.

### Saturday 20 April

It rained at one time during the night but only for a short period. Spent all day down in the cabins, reading or talking. Sat on the quarter deck for half hour. Had a nice bath and shower after tea.

It wasn't too warm on the flight deck but very close in the cabin. Had 6 bars of chocolate from the canteen. Wrote letters [home]. Went to pictures saw Kitty. Sleeping on the deck, clocks on ½ hour again (5½).

### Sunday 21 April (Easter Sunday)

Washed my white shorts. Ironed them after lunch, also shirt and the same for Ike Owens. After tea played deck hockey, lost 3–0, also Cudworth Cripples 4–2. Had a lovely blister, which was also busted, so I got a bath, and got it dressed... It's around the big toe.

### Monday 22 April (Easter Monday)

Arrived at Colombo at 6.20 in the morning. I sat up in bed to see everything as we entered the harbour. I was again sleeping on the side deck. But it was also raining heavily. It stopped about 7.30am. Had breakfast and got ashore at 9.20am. We were trying to get a bus to take us to candy for the day. But failed so we spent the morning looking around Colombo. Bought two sets of elephants. 3 in a set for 30/0 the lot. Bought a little necklace but I'm not keen on the chains 17/6.

Had dinner at the Globe Hotel not bad and met there again at 2pm. The town was very clean. But I think the outskirts or suburbs would be like Aden (dirty). We got a bus then from the Globe for Mount Lavinia, a quiet seaside place. It was lovely. We all went bathing, plenty of breakers, and all enjoyed ourselves. Had a cup of tea and a sandwich at the hotel by the beach.

Watched the people making lace, it looked simple, but takes some getting into.

Bought pineapples, they were lovely, also had bananas and coconuts. Got the bus back to the ship by 6.30pm. Had a bath, dinner, changed and went to a dance at the town hall. Most of the boys went, 7/6. But didn't have a dance as there were no 'excuse me's' and no women spare, all had come with their partners ... came back. Met Will Gaskin's boy on the jetty, he was on duty (Navy). It was he recognised me but I felt glad to have met him, got on board at 25 past 11, straight to bed. Got a letter.

**Tuesday 23 April**
Lovely day again, pulled out of the harbour for another carrier to pull in then at 8.30am, stopped astride till 12 noon. Slept for an hour up on the deck. Had tea, then got straight back to the bed where I read and chatted with the boys till it was dinner time, after which we went to the pictures and saw *The Dolly Sisters*. Not bad. I enjoyed it and so to bed. It was a bit cooler as well. It was nice watching the sun setting at 6.15pm. It seemed to set very quickly. Clocks on ½hour again (6 hours)

**Wednesday 24 April**
After breakfast there was Crossing the Line celebration, and the lot of us got a ducking, plenty of soap and flour, made like a paste, which was splashed on one's face. Then the chairs would tip backwards, and into the pool which was erected up on deck. From that one you got thrown to the other which only had a ... between the two. Bought two nail brushes at canteen.

Practised singing in the afternoon. Sung in a concert for the ratings at night. Had dinner, then went to the pictures. Saw *Wicked Lady*. Not a bad show. Clocks on ½hour (6½)

**Thursday 25 April**
The sea today is like a plate of glass, perfect, all flat, just a slight ripple. Wrote [letters]. Clocks on ½hour (7hours). Started training at 7.30am on flight deck.

**Friday 26th April**
Pay day again. Had a quiet day. Passed the Cocos Islands. Told at night we weren't supposed to sleep on the ... deck after tonight. Clocks on ½hour (7½ hours).

**Saturday 27 April**
Wrote [letters]. Didn't feel too good, the sea was a bit rough and while going to the mess for meals (which is well forward) we got full benefit of the rolling. So I just made a beeline for the cabin after all meals, and feel alright. Slept at the cabin. Weren't allowed on the deck. It was only for ratings, and we were lucky, as the whole deck got washed out with the waves, time after time. The sports on the flight deck weren't up to much. So I just watched it for 10 minutes. Went to bed at 8.15pm, but read till 9.25pm.

**Sunday 28 April**
Finished writing [letters]. Not quite so rough today. But my stomach is not quite settled, although I ate a good breakfast, everything finished off quite well. Got photo of the Welsh contingent of the touring team taken a week ago. Went to bed straight after dinner. Clocks on ½hour (8 hours). Wrote [letters].

**Monday 29 April**
A lot cooler today again, and a lot calmer. But since lunch it is starting to roll again. I shall be on the bed for a while reading again. Finished [letters]. Sea blowing up very rough.

**Tuesday 30 April**
Arrived Freemantle 10.20am. Went ashore and were received by the Mayor ... Given a cup of tea and sandwiches... a few speeches. Got driven to Perth. I had lunch. Played a game amongst ourselves at the Oval (exhibition), Went to Perth for the night. Went to the Tivoli variety, Jenny Howard (English comedienne) sang there. People of Freemantle took our addresses to send us home a parcel of food each. Met a Mr Seely (Oldham)

**Wednesday 1 May**
Walked around Freemantle. Had lunch (steak, egg, chips & salad). Bought brooches... Then went to Perth [shopping]

**Thursday 2 May**
Went training at the Oval Ground (Freemantle) had our usual lunch, then on to Perth. Went to Swamborn to look for friends of Mr James Travis (Oldham) but failed to find them. No such address and failed to check up ... even in the electoral roll. So went to Perth to meet the boys and finished off the day there.

**Friday 3 May**
Left the Indomitable (It's returning on Monday to England). And got moved to the Naval Barracks at ... just outside Freemantle. Went out with the boys at night to a pub. Left there at 9pm for a club where the Welsh people gather. But finished up at a dance. I got one dance. Then we all packed up and got a taxi home. It's very comfortable here. I've got a nice bed (Slumberland). But woke feeling very cold in the morning.

**Saturday 4 May**
Did training at 10.30am. Left at 1pm and went to Subiaco to see them play East Freemantle at home in their type of game, 18-a-side. Wasn't keen on it. Went on to Perth and had the usual lunch. Then went to Gloucester Park to see the trotting under floodlights, quite good. But only saw three races. ... Came back to camp after supper. There was a dance at the PO's mess. Had a dance, then to bed.

**Sunday 5 May**
Went training at 9.30am, then the whole day off. Did a lot of washing and ironing, went for a walk in the morning and tea-time. Then to the pictures at night in camp. ... Spent a lovely quiet day and much needed rest.

**Monday 6 May**
It rained, and although we had an invitation out to tea, they didn't turn up to fetch us. The young married couple we spoke to at the dance on Saturday at camp. So we stayed in till the afternoon (The team had gone on a tour for the day). Then went to the pictures in Freemantle, got back to camp... we were

leaving the following day so packed up all my kit. Went to a dance at night. It went fairly good, I danced a few times.

**Tuesday 7 May**
Got everything organised and left ... at 12.45pm, caught the troop train at Claremont, left there about 1.30pm.

**Wednesday 8 May**
We changed at Kalgoorlie. Had our first meal about 10.30 am. At the staging camp we changed trains for a line of a different gauge. Meals were cooked on the train and we just got out when the train stopped and got our food alongside. Just came across a few houses here and there, where the rail was double, for the sole purpose of refuelling or passing a train in the opposite direction. We had bunks at the stage of the journey, but not too comfortable.

**Thursday 9 May**
Nothing to report but the same as the day before, just passed a few houses. Went through the Nullabor Plain (nothing but sand) and also along the 300 straight stretch of rail.

**Friday 10 May**
Arrived and changed at Adelaide. Had a meal at the staging camp and went straight on overnight again without sleepers and one meal at a platform.

**Saturday 11 May**
Arrived at Melbourne at 1.30pm. handed all our travelling stuff (Blankets, cutlery, plate, tin) in the Navy ... Had a good meal in town, a lovely bath, another meal and back to the train. We travelled till 11pm when we changed.

**Sunday 12 May**
Stopped for breakfast in the way at a station, made a dash for it and were first in. It was run by the railway people. Arrived at last at Sydney at 1.20pm. A few people meeting us. But no bus, had to have taxis and pay ourselves. Had lunch, a bath and into bed. Dinner at 6pm. A little reception, then did a spot of writing and went for a walk with the boys. Ended up at the Phillip Street Club, then at British Centre and a dance. But only had one dance ...

**Monday 13 May**
Breakfast. It rained heavy. Then went to the broadcasting house. Did a little recording, but not much. Had a biscuit, then dinner and off to... to train at his gym. A few minutes in a sweat box and a good massage. Then tea next door, with Mr Williams (ex Carmarthen) and back to the hotel. Williams has a plantation of oranges and lemons, and has promised to send us some along. Went to the State Theatre... *Road to utopia*. I enjoyed it and have only just come back and am in bed. Had plenty of paper cuttings today.

**Tuesday 14 May**
Started our training on Sydney No.2 ground in the morning. Went to the home of a Welsh man from Glamorgan. Then back to lunch in his inn. Went to the Australian Broadcasting (ABC). Want to sing at a hospital week Friday. For

£21. The Welsh Choir. Went around the shops, bought braces (part elastic). Bought polo jersey. Ordered 6 pairs silk stockings, Davy Jones. Sent food parcel home from there. Back to dinner. Had letter from the manager of Murdock's stores (ex Oldham man), wants me to visit him. Went to the British Centre. But didn't dance. Saw the crest of various ships in the manager's office. Had ham & egg supper then back to bed.

### Wednesday 15 May
Did our training. Had photo of team taken on the Sydney ground. Lunch. Meeting on many particulars of New Zealand travel. Went to Murdock's store to see Mr Mallaline, the general manger. Showed us around part of the building where their material is made and also made up. Ordered ... 2 sets of pants and vests. Also a football jersey of the club's colours. Went with Ike to the ABC where they recorded him job training airborne. From there to the League Club where a reception was given for us, we were late. But OK. Stayed there drinking with this one and that one till 8.10pm. Then on to the British Centre, I didn't have a dance. But enjoyed myself as they were broadcasting a variety show from there, then home. Had 2lb butter given to me, but its loose, not tinned.

### Thursday 16 May
Went training early, finished at 10.30. Was on our way to see the Premier by 10.45. Had a reception there. Few sandwiches and drinks. Few photographs taken. Choir sang the usual songs (Welsh). Back to the hotel to lunch. Then away shopping. Got 7 pairs of silk stockings, and photo album at David Jones. Then back to dinner and stopped in writing [home].

### Friday 17 May
A very busy day from 10.45am. We left for a reception at the Lord Mayor's. After drinks and biscuits, back to lunch. Then Gus, Ike, Ted, Joe and myself went to the Minerva Theatre (which was playing *The Corn is Green* by Emlyn Williams) to see how things are set for us to sing with them in the show one night (Monday), when were their guests. Met people from all parts there, all speaking Welsh. It was grand. Hurried ... to go training at 2.30pm. Away again to reception at the Australian Hotel (equivalent to our Savoy). Plenty of food, ham turkey. No tables laid. Go and fetch your own as the chef plied it at a big and well laid table. Any amount of food. ... Mr Lord (ex Oldham), friend of Mr Hutchins.

After reception, went to a concert by the *Daily Telegraph* paper. The Choir sang *Bread of Heaven, Sospan Fach* on the air as we finished. Ted, Ike and myself were rushed away to the Labour broadcasting place. And broadcasting again, just a few answers to questions. We were taken there by Cuswer McGrath, the cartoonist. The reception was by the Consolidated Newspapers. Went there after we finished to see Ron Bye (photographer). Got a number of photos from him which he'd taken at various times.

Went from there to the British Centre. Had one dance, then back to the hotel and I felt dead tired. Received [letters].

**Saturday 18 May**
Trained in the morning. Saw the match between NS Wales and Queensland. NSW won. Went to the Welsh Society meeting, then on to Rockdale Town Hall to a dance.

**Sunday 19 May**
Went on a bus tour by … League Club. But it rained all day. 72mph gale at one time. Visit at … and Palm Beach. Got back for dinner at 6pm. Attended birthday party …

**Monday 20 May**
Training in the morning. Got the team's official photo taken in the afternoon. After dinner went to the Minerva Theatre and four of us sang … with the choir. Got called on the stage at the end of the show. It was good. Had a cup of tea and sandwiches with the cast.

**Tuesday 21 May**
Left Sydney 8.30am for Junee. Arrived there 5pm. The last miles in was a grand experience. For the engine driver blew his whistle and all the other engines in the sheds and sidings blew theirs in answer. On arriving the band was out. Big notices of "Welcome to Junee". Had a reception at railway refreshment room, then in bed by 10pm.

**Wednesday 22 May**
Got up at 6am. Mayor's reception early lunch, then changed at hotel and off to the field by bus. Won the game 36-4. After the game met a lot of people from Carmarthen who had been there about 20 years. Had to hitch hike from the ground, because the bus which had left the ground. Couldn't get back because of the crowd. Went to the ball at night. It finished at ¼ past 2 next morning.

**Thursday 23 May**
Got called by the manager at 8am. At 9 was on my way to a poultry farm. Saw oranges and lemons growing for the first time, had a lemon, and then a cup of tea and scones before leaving. Got some tinned fruit at a shop. Left at 11.40am. Crowds saw us leaving again and again the engine drivers played tunes on their whistles. Arrived in Sydney 9.20pm, had supper at a café, then hotel. A bath and to bed. But a few of they boys started talking, so didn't get to sleep till about 1am.

**Friday 24 May**
Trained morning. … Sent telegram to Ma to see if everything was alright because I hadn't received any mail. Had a massage at Longrushes. Bought two pyjamas (without coupons) also a pullover (white). Tonight the Welsh choir sang on the wireless … It went down alright and was in bed early. Saw one of the team photos in the *League … Review*. It's ok too.

**Saturday 25 May**
Trained at 9.30am. Out for lunch and dinner at the McGuinness and went to the rugby match at St George to see them against Eastern Suburbs. St George won 19–9. It was a glorious sunny day. Went to the pictures at night. Saw

Gary Cooper in a cowboy picture. But forget the name of it. Got 2 letters ... which arrived by ordinary mail.

### Sunday 26 May
Had a few photos of match at Junee. Wrote in the morning, sent photo of team [home] which I got out of *League News*. Went to Manly with Arthur Bassett.

### Monday 27 May
Got 3 letters, 2 by sea, one by air... Trained in the morning 10.30. Afternoon around town. Stopped in tonight writing. But went out at ¼ to 9, to Taylor's Corner for supper. It was delicious. Nice steak and onions, tomatoes, lettuce, got back at ¼ to 11.

### Tuesday 28 May
Went training in the morning, after lunch went to City Tattersall's Club to present Ashes Cup back to them. Went shopping bought 2 vests (silk) and a few coat hangers.

### Wednesday 29 May
Went to Canberra, played and won 45–12, got a bit of a jarring up and felt sore after the match. Couldn't sleep with the pain on the train, got to Sydney at 5.25 am Thursday. Met the Duke of Gloucester, also an officer Johnson of RAC (Aussie) going to take command out in Japan. Went to the Houses of Parliament, left at 8.30pm after dinner.

### Thursday 30 May
Went to Langrushes for heat and massage in morning, also afternoon. Went to the pictures at night.

### Friday 31 May
Massage morning and afternoon. Got a pair of greys and had a photo taken in them for the makers. Got a new pair of football boots.

### Saturday 1 June
Massage in morning. Match against NS Wales in the afternoon. Won 14–10. But win was dubious. The boys didn't play well at all, especially first half. They were very poor. I didn't play. Just strolled out at night. Got a bit of supper. Got an invite to a dance, but didn't go.

### Sunday 2 June
Went to Wollongong. Didn't play myself was making sure of the extra time off to be fit (fully). Met May Reason's sister-in-law, Mrs Barry, also husband and son (18). But didn't stop long with her. But took Wilf (husband) to the match. Got tickets for them, and people from Aberavon. ... We lost 15–12, were well beaten. Had an invite to spend a weekend any time I like. Had ... apples from the people. Parcel going home, left 8.20pm, got back 11.5pm and straight to bed.

**Monday 3 June**
Left at 8.35am from Central Station arrived Katoomba 12 noon. Had bus tour for an hour. Then to a hotel there for lunch. Left at 2.20pm by bus for Jenolan Caves, 53 miles away. It wasn't so great as it was raining heavily and cold. It also snowed on the way. Arrived at the Caves Hotel at 20 to 6pm. Had lunch, then at 7.30pm went around one of the many caves. It took two hours. Had supper. Then a dance or two. Only a piano was there, but it served the purpose.

**Tuesday 4 June**
Had a lovely night's sleep, got up at ¼ past 8. Had the morning free and saw them feeding Wallabies. Like small Kangaroos. Left after lunch approx 1.10pm. Got a train from Mt Victoria at 3.35pm. It is a glorious day. Got back to Sydney by 7pm. Got back to the hotel. Had a bath and into bed, wrote 2 letters.

**Wednesday 5 June**
Went training in the morning, shopping in the afternoon. Bought a trunk for £6/15/0, also pullover and silk stockings 5/- 4 pairs. Stopped in writing [home]. Sent 2 photos of the three Fred, Ike and myself, also the Welsh contingent taken on the ship.

**Thursday 6 June**
Went training in between heavy showers of rain. Had ... cancelled owing to the bad weather. Went and saw film of parts of last Saturdays' game. Bed in the afternoon, wrote a few letters. Went to "Boys Club" (Police BC). Then out to a house with ... for a few sandwiches and drinks. It was a lovely house everything modern and perfect. Had meeting and decided to fix curfew on ourselves for 11pm.

**Friday 7 June**
Training in the morning, wrote [letter] then went for a walk. Bought pair of white shoes for [present], had a quiet night. 2 Welsh men came here with Arthur Bassett. Both captains of cargo ships.

**Saturday 8 June**
Had an easy morning. Wilf Bray called with his son. Staying to see the match against NSW. We won 21–7. Went out to dinner after the match, then bed.

**Sunday 9 June**
Wrote a letter [home], went out about 11am to go to Wilf Bray's sister's house to dinner and tea. They were ... people and lived at Rockdale. Had home made Welsh cakes with her. Had a packet of cooking flour, all ready for use but for setting, left there at 6.30pm. Got back to the hotel by 7.15pm. Went out at 8pm to a concert. We were only there ... It went down ok and had a few drinks and sandwiches after at the house of one of the officials got home by 11.30pm.

**Monday 10 June**
Phoned Mrs Smith. Trying to get a coat [for a present] giving exact sizes.
Went out to the zoo for the afternoon (had to train in the morning). Went to
the pictures at night.

**Tuesday 11 June**
Left on 8.30 train for Orange, arrived at 3.20. Had an old Welsh man from
Ammanford to drive us to the Hotel. Had a civic reception at 4.15. Then dinner
at the ... Hotel where half the team stayed the other half at the Royal. The
food was quite good. Met a few Welsh ladies serving, who had been there for
17 years. The speeches were terrible. We walked out at 9pm. But it continued
till 10 or later. Orange was a grand town. Small, but clean and neat, bed by
10pm.

**Wednesday 12 June**
Took us up to the mountain top to see the place. It was lovey there, just like
home. From there to an orchard for mid-morning tea, plenty of cream, help
yourself. Won the match 33–2. Had dinner by the Welsh people. It was
intended for the Welsh lads only. But it extended to the team and English
people helped as well. It was held at the chapel house. Plenty of food. Never
eaten too much before of trifle and ice cream. Went to the dance afterwards.
It was grand. But had to leave early, caught the 10.45 train, had sleepers.

**Thursday 13 June**
Arrived in Sydney 7.30am taxi to hotel. Breakfast, packed some of my kit in
the trunk. Presents mostly. Had letters for [home] and my ... mail. Visited Boys
Town so was a grand place. Then went to Frank O'Rourke's for the evening
with Willie Davies and Alf Drewry.

**Friday 14 June**
Training in the morning. Visit to the glass works after dinner. Got a tumbler
with hand painting on it. My name also a couple dancing. Stopped in at night
writing. Got a few combs, ash tray in plastic and ... case. They made glass
cups at 34 per minute, small tumblers at 32 a minute. Stayed in at night
writing. Got my pair of rugby boots from Oldfields.

**Saturday 15 June**
Left Sydney 9am. Train for Newcastle, played and got sent off 20 minutes
before the end. Martin Ryan got carried off and had to have an operation for
rupture ... he pulled a muscle in the groin, got cautioned myself. Met an
Oldham man, gave me a few views of the city. Met an old Neath player Dai
Williams. Played for Ebbw Vale when they were playing rugby league. Had
dinner after the match and got the 7.20pm train back. Got into Sydney 11.20.
Got taxi to ... for a supper. Then back to the hotel, got a hot bath and into
bed.

**Sunday 16 June**
Mam's birthday. Had Turkish bath in the morning by Langridge's here at the
Australian Hotel. Strolled around Sydney in the afternoon, back to dinner and
stopped in writing.

**Monday 17 June**
Played in 1st test at Sydney Cricket Ground, Drew 8pts 8. Jack Kitching got sent off for fighting. There were 64,000 odd. We got share of the gate £10,000. Went to the ship Ocean Pride had a party on it, didn't get back until the early hours of morning. Feeling tired now.

**Tuesday 18 June**
Got my watch back, fixed up. Got letter from [home]. Had a bath in the morning, then packed up all kit to leave tonight at 9.10 for Tamworth.

**Wednesday 19 June**
Arrived Tamworth at 8.30am. Breakfast at station hotel, fairly cold weather, walked around the town, bought bed jacket [as present], went to the Town Hall reception, also bus ride, visited Agricultural University. Had tea and cakes there. Didn't want lunch at hotel before match. Won 61 to 5. Scored one try. Had dinner after the match, also went to a ball. Had supper there after being introduced to the public on the stage, left at 11pm. Got into the sleeper, got to bed straight away, slept well.

**Thursday 20 June**
Got up about 7.30, little snow about. Changed trains and had breakfast at 8.30am. Tea and sandwiches at 12.30, then dinner at 3.30. Each time in the station refreshment rooms, arrived in Brisbane 8. Had dinner at station, then bus to hotel, not much comfort here. But won't be long here owing to travelling and playing so much. 5 of us in one room, Ike, Frank, Arthur and Ted.

**Friday 21 June**
Had tea in bed at 7.15. After breakfast went training on the Brisbane Cricket Ground. Strolled around town till lunch. Wrote a few letters and posted them. Had a Welcoming Reception at the Hotel at 4pm. Had airmail. Had 11 letters, feeling on top of the world with them. Wrote [home] after dinner and so to bed.

**Saturday 22 June**
Sent the parcels home … Saw film of 1st test match. Lost our match against Queensland 25–24. After dinner went to the Welsh Society. It was a good do. Also had our photos taken there. 9 of us. Had tea and cake there, also Welsh cakes. From there to the Kangaroos dinner. Got back to the hotel 20 past 12. Gave two addresses to Eddie Waring for someone sending parcels home …

**Sunday 23 June**
Did morning writing, had phone call from Oldham boy, Ron Deaden, Chatterton Rd. After lunch went to a place called Lone Pine to see Koala bears and Kangaroos. Had a few photos taken by press and Bryn Knowelden. Back for dinner, wrote [home]. Then caught the 9.0pm train, had sleepers.

**Monday 24 June**
Arrived Bundaberg at 10.00, party split up into 3 hotels. Am in the Hotel Bundaberg myself. Went training in the morning. Found out I was having a

rest from the game here. After lunch went to a beach with coconuts growing alongside. Then to a sugar cane plantation, had afternoon tea there after getting dinner went out to the pictures and saw *Captain Kidd*.

## Tuesday 25 June
Strolled around town, had 2 tins of pineapples. Had a bit of a Civic Reception by the Mayor. ... quiet for a change. Had a good lunch, then went to the match against Wide Bay. Won 16–10. But it wasn't a good game to watch. Very dusty, like a coal tip. Glad I wasn't playing. Went to a dance at night. Lovely floor.

## Wednesday 26 June
Left Bundaberg at 9.15am and arrived at Rockhampton at 10.30pm, which is only a distance of 179 miles. Got food at the station. Left at 11.15pm, got split up into 3 hotels, ours being the Normandy. It was filthy and started scratching as soon as I got there. Slept there and moved out the following morning

## Thursday 27 June
Bought a grey pullover 11/6. Played the game and won 35–12. Scored a try. Went to a dance at night. Oil lamps they had burning there. Lights electric put out at 9pm. Dance was poor, so got back at 11.10 at the hotel only got there at 9.05.

## Friday 28 June
Left Rockhampton at 8.45am for Townsville. Got our meals laid on at various stations, very poor tea. No sleepers but slept on the floor. ... way to spend one's birthday. [Phillips was 27]

## Saturday 29 June
Arrived Townsville at 6am. Straight to the hotel. Bath into bed but couldn't sleep. So got up for breakfast. Strolled around very hot and close. But as cooling off slightly ... went training after lunch. And again the sun came out. Very hot. Walked about in shirt sleeves, strolled as far as the beach after training. Went in paddling to watch 3 men fishing with a net, then back for dinner and went to the pictures. Saw *Gentle Set* and *The power of a whistle* then bed. Gave ... name for address to a parcel.

## Sunday 30 June
Had a good night's rest. Got up at ¼ past 8. Short walk after breakfast, then back for a shower and more writing. Played and won by 55–16. Had a quiet night, went walking.

## Monday 1 July
Went to Magnetic Island half hour by boat off Townsville. Picked coconuts, had lunch there and left at 1.15. Back at the hotel. Got picked up to leave at 4pm by plane for Mackay. Arrived at Mackay at 25 past 6. Took 1 [hour] 35 minutes actually flying. Had dinner, then went to the pictures. The first picture house with deckchairs inside (double width).

122

**Tuesday 2 July**
Played Mackay and broke all records. Won 94 – nil. Dance at night. Not bad. But good floor. Visited harbour in the morning.

**Wednesday 3 July**
Bought … for gifts for home. Left at 5.4pm by plane for Brisbane. Arrived at Hotel from airfield at 10 past 10pm. Got straight to bed. It was a good trip, conditions grand. Received 13 letters on arrival here.

**Thursday 4 July**
Went training in the morning, wrote letters after dinner. Went for a walk to post them and buy more letters (Air). Went to pictures after tea. But wasn't much good. Came out. Had cup of tea, then bed at 10pm after a lovely bath.

**Friday 5 July**
Bought a [present]. … Got telegrams … Ordered photos from paper for nothing. Have also asked Wilf Corbett to order 1 doz. Group photos and 3 lined up photos of the team for when we'll get back to Sydney for presents. Went to pictures at night. Saw *Son of Lassie*. Good show, marvellous dogs.

**Saturday 6 July**
Went around town in the morning. Had a massage. Early lunch then laid down for a rest. Played and won the 2nd test at Exhibition Ground Brisbane. Had a bottle party in the room after dinner then went to a dance in the Town Hall.

**Sunday 7 July**
Went out as guests of the Governor by car to a place called Southport 60 miles away. Lovely seaside. Grand for swimming. Saw exhibition of it and life saving. Back by dinner time. Wrote a few letters and in bed by 10 to 10.

**Monday 8 July**
Mayor's reception in the morning at City Hall. Went to Tattersall's Club with Bill Kenny. Had lunch there, back to Parliament House. Went through it, had tea and drinks there, also ice cream. Back for dinner, then in bed early before 10pm.

**Tuesday 9 July**
Went strolling in the morning. Played in the afternoon against Brisbane, won 21–15. Went with Bill Kenny to his house, had dinner there and left at 10.20pm. Had tea in café opposite and to bed 11.15.

**Wednesday 10 July**
Had massage at Gabba ground and went from there to Stock Exchange Club. Had a few drinks then back for lunch. Went with Arthur Bassett shopping intending to get butter promised us. But will get it on Friday. Also put parcel each sent home for us. Spent afternoon there, too late to shop so got back. Wrote a few letters, had dinner. Then a bath and more letters, posting them and then to bed.

**Thursday 11 July**
Went to Ipswich. Had a reception by Mayor. Also Welsh folks. Didn't play. But won the match 21–12. Had a dinner after the match, then straight back. Got here ¼ past 10.

**Friday 12 July**
Got book of Australia from general manager …. Out to lunch. Got box of chocolates each. Went shopping with Arthur Bassett. Bought [presents]. Saw picture of 2nd test at News theatre. Went to a Mr & Mrs Warren's place for a party. A section of the Welsh contingent. They gave us a good time, real good night, plenty of singing.

**Saturday 13 July**
Left for Toowoomba at 8.45am arrived 12.20 had lunch then the match. We won 34–5. Went to the dinner after, then to the dance for 1½ hours. Got to the bus at 10pm. But others … left at 11.20. 2 of the group behind Ted Ward and Gus Risman. Got here at Brisbane 2.20am Sunday. Bought cardigan.

**Sunday 14 July**
Morning of letter writing. Spent afternoon in the park listening to the band. Back for dinner at 6pm then a short walk around. Met the … (Welsh) they gave us 2 kitbags. Gave one to Arthur Bassett. So managed to get all my things packed away.

**Monday 15 July**
Left at 11am after buying [presents]. The boys left at Grafton for game there. 8 of us carried on for Sydney. Travelled all night without sleepers.

**Tuesday 16 July**
Arrived Sydney 8.15am. Got luggage of team together and on the bus. Then for the hotel. Got breakfast at 9.30. Had a lovely bath then sorted myself out and wrote. After lunch, went around the shops. Had an early night.

**Wednesday 17 July**
Went training in the morning, around shops, bought photo of team group for Mam's Ma and long one for Oldham. Did my packing, put most of the things in my trunk. Didn't go out after dinner at 6pm.

**Thursday 18 July**
Visited the people at Manly. Really felt at home. Trained in the morning, bought photos of team from the *Sun* paper. Bought [presents].

**Friday 19 July**
Ordered more photos. Back for lunch, then went out to Mrs Smith's, Mrs Barry, Wilf and Don were also there … spent the afternoon there and evening, left on the 9pm train.

**Saturday 20 July**
Got the other photos I ordered. Then back to write. Met a Les Davies at the hotel, an old workmate of Freddie Newton of Sidney terrace. He was from Swansea. Played in 3rd test, won 20–7. Spent evening at Manly.

**Sunday 21 July**
Could have spent the night at Manly. Harry wanted to show me around the Surf Club. But had promised the Puddicombe family (which I met at Orange) to go out there for the day. Went at 10.30am to Greenwich, and spent an enjoyable day there. Went out by car in the afternoon and got back to the hotel at 20 to 10pm. Did a bit more packing. Finished off my trunk.

**Monday 22 July**
Went to Langridge's for electric massage. Shopping in the afternoon. Ordered photo of presentation of the Ashes. Went to the State Theatre at night, saw the film *Smithy*. I enjoyed it.

**Tuesday 23 July**
Finished packing, put trunk and blue case down to be loaded on the ship (taken from hotel by lorry) after lunch sent telegram to Harry and wife, they were being married. Had haircut. Collected photos ordered Monday. Went to manly. They were waiting with me with a taxi. They'd been married, and had a few drinks while waiting for me before returning home. Had a good laugh over the telegrams. Gave them my address for them to send ... home to us. When I got back at the Olympic the place was full. Got to bed at 20 to 2 Wednesday.

**Wednesday 24 July   New Zealand**
Got up at 5 to 4am, went out at 4.30 for Rose Bay, the flying boat berth. Left there at ¼ to 6 and arrived at Auckland NZ at ¼ past 2pm. The clocks are 2 hours in advance here again. Had a stroll around then dinner and straight to bed to write.

**Thursday 25 July**
Tea in bed. Got up at 5 to 8. Good food at this hotel, Royal. Went training in the morning. The field was very muddy. Went around the shops after lunch. Bought pairs of socks [and presents].
    Went to pictures at night, and saw the *Seventh Veil*. I enjoyed it. Had tea and toast after, then to bed. But it was on midnight after packing up for the morning.

**Friday 26 July**
Had breakfast at 8am. Left at 9.15am. But on arriving at the air office found we were too early. Left there at 10am, 21 miles to the [aero]drome, left there at 12 noon. Arrived at Christchurch at ¼ to 3. Putting up at United Services Hotel. Very good. Had a few words over the wireless, intended going to the dance. But felt too tired after sitting in the lounge talking.

**Saturday 27 July**
Not playing today. The ground was very muddy at one end but we managed to win 24–12. Wrote a few letters and left the hotel at 9pm. Then left the station at 9.35. No sleepers.

**Sunday 28 July**
Arrived at Greymouth, 5.25am. Went to bed by ¼ to 6. Slept till ¼ past 12 noon. Got up for lunch. The majority of the boys had gone out on a sight seeing trip, But it was a bad day. It rained all the time. After lunch an old gent invited us out for a ride around in his car. We went about 80 miles. Passed many gold mines, and where they had worked gold, also timberlands. Back in time for lunch, then at night went to the pictures which had been laid on for us. But they weren't so good. Got to bed at 11pm.

**Monday 29 July**
Got up at 8.30. Tea in bed at 7. Had breakfast, then a short walk. Bought pairs of shoes with straps and buckle fasteners. Also cheap bedroom slippers. Had a Mayor's reception. Played against West Coast (of South island). The ground was very muddy from one end to the other. But we lost 17–8. dance at night. Met a woman from Treherbert, been here 18 years. At the hotel with Dai Jenkins.

**Tuesday 30 July**
Left Greymouth 10.30am. Got lunch on the way. Arrived at Christchurch, had dinner at 6pm. Left by train for Lyttleton for boat across to Wellington. It was a very rough trip. But was fortunate enough to go to sleep without being … although I wasn't far off.

**Wednesday 31 July**
Arrived Wellington 7.30am. Went straight to various hotels. I landed at Barretts, not bad. But not extra. Met woman from Taranaki who knew … Beynon (Mrs Fraser). Played against the Maoris and won 32–8. Got a kick on the thumb, had it X-rayed. But nothing broken. But very sore. Couldn't use it. Went to the pictures at night. Played against Bramley who played with me with the Army team in Germany last October. He's demobbed. Also a few chaps there who knew me. But didn't stop. I asked how Catterick went on.

**Thursday 1 August**
Walked around Wellington in the morning. Left at ¼ to 3 for Auckland

**Friday 2 August**
Arrived Auckland 7am. Went straight to the Royal Hotel. Went walking after writing a few letters. Pictures at night.

**Saturday 3 August**
Played Auckland. But was out of it myself and very lucky so. For it was the biggest mudbath I'd ever seen. Had a job to distinguish our boys from the opponents. We won. I felt like going to the dance or pictures. But after talking I went to bed at 9.30pm.

### Sunday 4 August

Left at 9.30am by bus for Rotorua. Stopped at Huntley for a cup of morning tea, supplied by the ladies supporters club. Had lunch at Hamilton. But it wasn't very good. Although the hotel was grand. Carried on got to Rotorua at 6.30pm (180 miles) had a bath and dinner, did some writing. Did a bit of massaging of Ike Owens's leg. It had gone up after a kick on Saturday.

### Monday 5 August Bank Holiday

Visited a Maori settlement ... for sightseeing. Saw the two Geysers blowing forth steam about 80ft high. Saw people washing and cooking in natural hot water pools, in the afternoon went for a bus ride, and at night played Housey Housey [Bingo]. Went to a Maori Concert.

### Tuesday 6 August

Went to a certain spot by bus, then walked through land which had been interrupted by volcanic eruption years ago (1886)? approx. Saw the longest boiling post. It was a grand sight, a lovely ... Crossed two lakes by motor launch (lakes created by eruption. Bought a few souvenirs, books of views, also a pencil case with Maori carvings on it. Back to hotel for dinner. The bus waited the other side of the lakes for us.) At night went to the pictures saw *Music for Millions.*

### Wednesday 7 August

Left Roratura at 9am. Stopped at Hamilton for half hour. Bought pairs of bed slippers for mam and myself, the same type. Went on to Huntley. Again I didn't play, owing to my thumb not being right. But it was a good game, we won. Had dinner at night, also a dance. But had to leave after an hour to get back to Auckland (80 miles). Got there at midnight. Had lunch at Princess Te peak (Maori).

### Thursday 8 August

Went training on Carlaw No.2 But it was in a bad state, my first run out since playing at Wellington. Had met an ex Oldham player, George ... (Scot) living at Napier. Came to see me, also Busty (mate of Bramley's) who also played with me in Germany. Also Alan Laird (NZ who played for Oldham while stationed at home in the NZ RAF) and an ex Oldham man living out there, George Howarth. Got me lard and dripping, freshly tinned, also soap and sugar, also gave me a present of cuff-links in ... shell, mounted in silver.

### Friday 9 August

Had met previous Saturday girl from Pontypridd who married a NZ RAF boy, nice fellow. Mel Painter her name was. Carmen Thomas, she was browned off. Been there two years. Went to their place for dinner, Arthur Bassett, Ike Owens and myself. They lived in a staging camp. She was a midwife and was at first nursing at a hospital at Halifax, where Arthur got to know her, and she phoned him up. But he was out. I spoke to her. She was excited at speaking Welsh again. Went to pictures at night.

### Saturday 10 August
Played the test, was left out of it. But it was lost 13–8. We played the wrong type of game. Did not suit the weather or field. It rained all the time. Went to pictures again at night. It rained nearly all day. The picture house was called the Civic. It was like being in the open air, stars above, also clouds passing over, affected by lights, marvellous sight.

### Sunday 11 August
Went for a stroll around Devonport, just a ferry ride away, faced Auckland. But it turned out very miserable, so back we went. Spent the night in writing.

### Monday 12 August
Did a bit of final shopping ... a few presents. Played in the match which was extra and we won 22–9? The referee was wicked. But changed at half-time (Someone must have spoken to him) If not we would have lost for every time we got near their line we were penalised, also near our own line. Went to pictures that night again. Plenty more rain. Sent a parcel [home].

### Tuesday 13 August
Final walk around, packing, had to buy another kit bag. Terrific weight in them with tinned food, also ... (14 lbs). Hope I get it ashore. Left Auckland at 7.10pm for Wellington. Got cup of tea at station, many waiting for us. Tea and pies really for the Welsh 5, also packet of sugar and large tins of beef dripping. Also ... we had lunch with members of the Welsh Society and one gave me a few tins of food, tongue, corned beef, honey. Was lucky, had a sleeper. We drew lots for them, as only 16 were available.

### Wednesday 14 August
Were late getting in. 11.30am were due at 9.15am. Went straight on board HMS Rangitiki, sailed at 3.15pm was quite calm.

### (2) Thursday 15 August
Of these we had two days. The first time ever known it. Instead of putting the clocks back, we went back a day, and put them on. It was very rough these few days but managed to keep my own, only few of the group were sick.

### Friday 16 August
Again rough, the ship kept bobbing up and down, like a bottle.

### Saturday 17 August
Should have held a dance at night but owing to rain and rough seas had pictures in the lounge, weren't bad either.

### Sunday 18 August
A bit calmer, strong breeze, did quite abit of pacing the deck. Went to church service, spent quiet day.

### Monday 19 August
Very much the same weather, had an impromptu concert that night, team sang. On the whole it was quite good. The resistance these brides and

fiancées put on at first is breaking down, they're speaking to different people. A thing which has to be, on a small holding like this ship.

**Tuesday 20 August**
Weather again the same, played Housey Housey at night.

**Wednesday 21 August**
Weather starting to improve. But still very dubious. Keen wind up. Had dance at night in the open, but ship rolled too much. It was very difficult at times, going up and down hill.

**Thursday 22 August**
Weather not too good. Housey Housey at night.

**Friday 23 August**
Weather a bit better. Did a bit of sun bathing. Intend to get very brown before getting home. Quiet night, horse racing on top deck.

**Saturday 24 August**
A lovely day, slight breeze. But still very warm. Lay in shorts all day, reading up to now, have met various people, some Welsh one Llanelli girl going back home, 2 children, girl of Bridgend, going home after visiting people of her ex fiancé, who she was going to get married to. But he was killed, … going to Pembroke, and others all over the country. Had dance on top deck. It was very good, with a slight breeze. Played my game in deck tennis competition. Won.

**Sunday 25 August**
Had news that we were going to New York to disembark the USA passengers, everybody pleased. Hope we can get ashore. Had a day in the sun again, in shorts, very quiet, had a quiet sing song, just a few of us.

**Monday 26 August**
Very breezy. But sun up quite warm. A slight change in weather again, ship beginning to roll. Concert at night.

**Tuesday 27 August**
Very windy, and fairly chilly. Taking a quiet day, talk of playing in New York. But not definite yet. Went to the pictures. Saw *Half Way House*, fairly good.

**Wednesday 28 August**
Weather still a bit rough. Eased a bit for the dance at night. But only records were played. It was more or less a flop.

**Thursday 29 August**
Quite nice in the morning and early afternoon. Strong breeze. Played deck tennis, but got knocked out of the competition. Went cold after and caught something in the stomach, which kept me moving from 5pm till 11pm. But ok after got to bed at 8.30pm.

**Friday 30 August**
Still very breezy. Got the team photos of the League (Mr Gabbatt). Had a quiet day for £5 (NZ) also our pay £1.00 Sterling.

**Saturday 31 August**
Strong breeze had died down quite a bit. Did a spot of sun bathing. Had a sports in the afternoon, didn't partake in it myself, enjoyed looking on. Saw the tennis semi-final. Very good game (Martin Ryan and partners). Quite a good dance at night.

**Sunday 1 September**
Very warm in the morning, (in the tropical sun). Saw the tennis final. A good game, but it rained, and it was spoilt, cleared up ok after. Had a quiet singsong at night. Early bed, very close. Laid on the clothes, did sleep ok. Posted letters [home], 2/- airmail stamps.

**Monday 2 September**
Very warm first thing, had rain at 11.30 ... very heavy shower. Sighted land at 12.15 noon. Opened trunk, placed large group photo in and retied. Arrived at Panama Bay at 9pm. Anchored up. Immigration officer came abroad.

**Tuesday 3 September**
Left Bay at 6am got the first lock at 8.30am. Berthed at Cristobal near Colon at 3.30pm. Went ashore and bought 2 pairs nylons. Went to a cabaret (Florida) got back to the ship at 11.30. Boat left at 12.30 9after midnight). Got in just before a tropical storm broke and watched the others come aboard in the rain.

**Wednesday 4  September**
Got to bed at 1.15am. Terrific thunder and lightening. Nearest I've been to lightening and it made me move. I thought it landed on the ship, but apparently it landed just behind. Very tired trying to get up. Lightening did hit ship, had slight fire in wireless room (curtains on fire). Went to the dance on top deck. Very quiet there.

**Thursday 5 September**
Very hot day. Spent it sun bathing, went to horse racing at night, sighted land and ships, which was approx 60 miles from Caracas.

**Friday 6 September**
Arrived Caracas at 5.30am. Got up at ¼ to 8. Went ashore at 10am. Bought two watches (wristlet) ... got back at 12.30 noon. Didn't go out after. Were due back to sail at 3pm. But didn't sail till 3.50pm. Had a quiet night (Very hot, hottest yet)

**Saturday 7 September**
Very hot during the day. Did quite a bit of washing clothes, also ironing. Had dance at night. It went very well, better than usual.

**Sunday 8 September**
Sea rough, heavy rain. Did the remainder of my ironing. Turned out a lovely evening.

**Monday 9 September**
Very warm, sea moderate, but had to keep ports closed at 8pm. Had ladies sports and did a bit of sun bathing. Pictures at night.

**Tuesday 10 September**
A lovely scorching day. Had a few games of tennis. News of ship diverting to Halifax, Nova Scotia, Canada instead of New York. Had a dance at night also a few people dressed up, in various clothing. Quite a good laugh.

**Wednesday 11 September**
The weather was terrific. Undoubtedly the hottest day of the tour. There was a concert and picture show arranged at night. But finally only the pictures took place with the presentation of prizes (money) for the sports that had taken place on the trip. The picture was very old (A Shirley Temple, when she was a child) The wind started to rise. So went for a cup of tea, with the girl going to Pembroke.

**Thursday 12 September**
A big change in two days. It rained a bit during the night and was fairly breezy all day. People were in their woollens again. I stopped in ... night time. Arrived at Halifax at 9.20pm. But on arrival had to put watches on one hour. So it read 20 past 10. No one was allowed ashore, except the fiancés and brides for America. They were due to leave in a train at midnight. But were still there early morning and some of the girls were still on board because their bonds had not come through.

**Friday 13 September**
Saw about a dozen of the girls hanging about. Got ashore ourselves about 9.30 to 10am. The weather was quite mild. Bought some tin foods. Two thermos flasks, scrap book, baby's cosy cover, two zip jackets, brooch and ear rings. The town was very cheap and plenty of everything there. Would liked to have presents all round. But it was impossible, they were too many. Received [letters]. Came back to the ship for meals, went to the wrestling match, it was my first. Had a few good laughs. But don't like wrestling. We got complimentary seats. Got back about 10 past 11pm and went straight to bed. Met chap at the gang way. He played with Stan Bowes (Cardiff & Navy) in the Navy. I think his name was Commons.

**Saturday 14 September**
Left Halifax early morning, 20 past 12am. The sea is pretty rough. All ports had to be closed water still came through and had to tighten them up during the night. We're on our last stage home. "The last Hop." No dance, weather too rough. Had pictures and Tombola. Went to the latter. But didn't win.

**Sunday 15 September**

Very foggy and it was very close so I got into shorts for a few hours. I went to service in the morning, played a few games of deck tennis. Played off my quoits and lost in our tournament amongst the team.

**Monday 16 September**

Still foggy, the fog horn was only sounded occasionally, whereas yesterday it was on nearly all day. ... lovely around tea time. Concert at night, it went pretty good. Had heavy following wind.

**Tuesday 17 September**

Sea still very choppy with a following wind, so again today, like yesterday, we should make very good time. Heard we'll be in Tilbury at 11am Sunday. Hope I'll get home that day. Mileage very disappointing, only did 336 miles per 24 hours. Went to Housey Housey. Won a straight house, £1/7/6.

**Wednesday 18 September**

This was the original date of approx arriving in England. But here we are still 4 days out a t sea, one of the engines stopped for a few hours. But got going again at 12 noon. Have spent the past few days reading a book called Green Years. It's been raining all day today. So I've spent most of my time in the dormitory. Had a quiet night, in bed early.

**Thursday 19 September**

Still very rough, rained off and on. But not heavy, very misty, visibility fair, cleared up at night, still a strong following wind. Went to Housey, Housey, no luck.

**Friday 20 September**

... Sent telegram of revised arrival (Sunday midnight ... back Monday) and birthday greetings. Grand day, very clear sunny with a bit of wind. The best day since leaving Halifax. Dance at night. But ship is rolling, so it won't be very enjoyable. I'm just going off to finish my packing. Put my big trunk into the baggage room one deck higher, got all the team's luggage together. So that will go off in one heap with the hope of keeping it likewise and save trouble when loading into a lorry at Tilbury which is taking it to our respective stations. We're having a bus. Will be quicker than the special train (I hope). Might be able to catch the midday train.

This is the last diary entry. The team finally arrived at Tilbury on 22 September at 10pm. Doug Phillips resumed his rugby league career with Oldham on 2 October, in a Lancashire Cup tie at Leigh.

# Appendix: The Lions players

N.B. As far as we are aware, at the time of writing, only Joe Egan and Bryn Knowelden are still alive.

**Gus Risman** Captain. Centre.
*Weight 13 stone. Height 5 feet 10 inches.*
*Born: 21 March 1911. Died: 17 October 1994*
Augustus John Risman was born in the Tiger Bay area, where his parents ran the seaman's mission. He was spotted by Frank Young, a rugby league scout, who arranged with Lance Todd, the New Zealander who was manager of Salford, to give the 17 year old a trial. Cardiff rugby union club were interested him, as were Tottenham Hotspur. Gus joined Salford as a full-back or centre.

He had the longest career in professional rugby league, making his debut for Salford on 31 August 1929 and 25 years and four months later played his final match for Batley. He played 873 matches, kicked 1,678 goals and scored 232 tries amassing 4,052 points. He was 41 when he received the Challenge Cup at Wembley in 1952 captaining Workington Town who beat Featherstone Rovers 18–10.

He played for Salford at Wembley when they beat Barrow in 1938, and captained Salford in three Championship wins, the Challenge Cup once, Lancashire Cup four times, and they were Lancashire League winners five times. Gus was the guiding genius behind the side, and also regularly accompanied Lance Todd on scouting missions to Wales enabling the club to have a regular stream of talent from the Valleys.

On returning to Britain after the Indomitables tour he joined Workington Town as player-coach. They had only been in the Rugby League for one year and badly needed a guiding hand to lead a side of promising young players. In his eight years as player-coach at Workington they became a team to fear, winning the Championship and Challenge Cup. He played 301 games for them, kicking 717 goals and scoring 33 tries.

His representative career began in 1930 representing Glamorgan and Monmouthshire in a 14–10 victory over Yorkshire. He scored a try playing at centre. Four months later he played his first match for Wales, against England, the first of 18 Welsh caps. He also represented England against France in 1934 in Paris.

As a Lions player he started on the 1932 tour, initially as understudy to the legendary Jim Sullivan, playing 17 times. He was selected for the 1936 tour, and captained the Lions for the first time in the third test which saw them retain the Ashes. The 1946 tour was his international finale.

When he finally retired as a player he initially coached Salford for four year before moving to Oldham, and finally Bradford. Gus had two sons, Bev and John, who both made a major contribution to the game.

**Tommy McCue** Vice-Captain Scrum-half
*Age 32 years. Deceased.*
*Weight 11 stone 8 pounds. Height 5 feet 6 inches*
Tommy was a product of the famous Widnes school St Bede's and as a schoolboy was seen as something special. He signed for Widnes in 1930 from a famous junior club, Manchester Ship Canal.

He played in two Wembley Challenge Cup Finals for Widnes, the first in 1934 when they lost to Hunslet. The second was in 1937 when he gave a man-of-the-match performance, scoring one try himself and creating two others. By this time he had already represented Great Britain at home and was an outstanding tourist in 1936.

The Second World War saw him turn out quite regularly as a guest player for Halifax. In 1945–46, he guided Widnes to their first ever Lancashire Cup Final win, against Wigan, who were overwhelming favourites. The match was played at Warrington before a crowd of 28,184.

He was a player who opened the game for others to score, but rarely appeared on the scoring chart. He made six appearances for Great Britain between 1936 and 1946,

11 appearances for England between 1935 and 1946, and never scored a try. He was the only player not to score a point on the 1946 tour, and while his team mates were desperate to see him score it did not bother him at all.

He was at the height of his powers during the 1946 tour, and certainly the way he guided the tourists in the first test, when they played the whole second half with 12 men, marked him out as a player of sheer genius. The war years did no favours to such as Tommy, as he would have been at his peak in that period. Certainly, the whole of Australia saw, and respected him as the greatest half-back in the world at that time. He had lost some of his speed by this stage, but instead of scoring would set up team mates for tries.

### Arthur Bassett Winger

*Born 28 June 1914. Died 30 December 1999.*
*Weight: 12 stone 12 pounds. Height 5 feet 10½ inches.*

Arthur was born at Kenfig Hill, Bridgend in 1914. He had a meteoric rise through the junior ranks in Welsh rugby union, and by the time he was 19, was selected for the national side against Ireland in March 1934. He won a further five Welsh caps, but missed out on a British Lions tour to South Africa in 1938. His elder brother Jack was another famous Welsh international, but played at full back.

Arthur was approached by several rugby league clubs in 1934, but being in the police force he was given time off for rugby tours, including with the British Police side. After his disappointment in 1938 over not being selected for the Lions, Halifax stepped in to sign him for £999. This odd amount arose because of a bet between a Halifax director, and a Leeds one, that Halifax could sign Arthur for less than £1,000. Arthur received the extra pound separately.

Such was the interest in his signing, over 5,000 watched his 'A' team debut, and he rapidly earned the nickname Blue Streak. He assisted Halifax in winning the 1939 Challenge Cup by beating Salford 20–3. Due to all the excitement of the cup run, Arthur's transfer to a West Riding police force was overlooked. With the start of war imminent, a rugby loving chief constable from Derbyshire stepped in, and added Arthur to the Derbyshire Constabulary. He made less than 50 appearances for Halifax during the war years, but regularly turned out for Nottingham rugby union club. The 1946 Lions tour was the peak of Arthur's rugby league international career.  He won two rugby league caps for Wales.

Due to travel difficulties, living in Derbyshire, Halifax let him go to York in 1948, after he had scored 66 tries in 110 appearances. He finally retired from the game in 1950, after playing mainly at loose-forward with York. After leaving the police he was a publican, and then became head of security at Chatsworth House, guarding some of the nation's greatest treasures.

### Eric Batten Winger

*Born 1914. Believed to have died in 1993.*
*Weight 12 stone 2 pounds. Height 5 feet 9½ inches*

Eric was the second son of the legendary Billy Batten, who was among the first inductees of the Rugby League Hall of Fame, and certainly Eric must be a serious candidate for this honour. Like his father, Eric was born at Kinsley near Hemsworth, a mining area of the West Riding of Yorkshire. An area known for breeding league players, and if they did not make it, became Yorkshire County cricket players.

He was one of those players who seemed to go on forever. His career started in 1933 until finally retiring in 1954. His clubs included Wakefield Trinity, Hunslet, Leeds and Featherstone Rovers, the latter as player-coach. He signed for Bradford in 1943, and played for them until 1951, where the majority of the game's honours came his way. In that period he scored 165 tries for Bradford alone. In his total career he totalled 443 tries from 630 appearances. Four times, he was the League's leading try scorer, twice with Hunslet, 1939–40 and 1942–43, and twice with Bradford, 1944–45 and 1945–46. He was known as the 'man of granite'.

Besides his three Great Britain caps on the 1946 tour, he won a further one against New Zealand in 1947. He was an integral part of that Bradford trophy winning side of the forties, winning two Challenge Cup winners medals, and one runner up medal, plus Yorkshire Cup and Yorkshire League medals. He won 13 England caps scoring 6 tries. He would tear down the wing at full speed, and then leap over a defender to score, something not seen in the modern game.

He retired as a player in 1954, but continued to coach Featherstone Rovers, and then coached at Batley.

### George Curran Prop

*Age 23. Died 29 December 1988.*
*Weight 13 stone 3 pounds. Height 5 feet 10 inches.*
George was born in Wigan, and signed for Salford from Whelley Central School in 1937. He made his first team debut at St Helens on 19 October 1940. He guested for Wigan in 1941, and then with Dewsbury from 1942 to 1944 alongside Salford's Gus Risman.

He was an ideal player for a tour party, being able to play in every forward position, and while he was the reserve hooker on the 1946 tour, he only regularly played in that position with Salford when Bert Day left in 1948. George made 175 appearances for Salford, scoring 12 tries, and one goal. His last game for the club was on 30 September 1950 at Keighley, before he transferred to Wigan for £2,000. Although he did not have any club success during his period with Salford, his international appearances were not diminished. As well as his two caps on tour; he represented Great Britain four more times, from 1946 to 1949 represented England 12 times and Lancashire on seven times. At Wigan he played 63 games, scoring eight tries.

The game's honours came to him towards the end of his career. With Wigan he won a Challenge Cup medal in 1951. At the end of that year he moved on to Huddersfield, winning a Challenge Cup medal in 1953, and a Yorkshire Cup winner's medal. He played 92 times for Huddersfield, scoring three tries. A hand injury at work forced him to retire from playing in 1954.

### Willie Davies Half Back

*Born: 28 March 1916. Died: 26 September 2002*
*Weight 11 stone. Height 5 feet 8 inches.*
William Thomas Harcourt Davies was born in 1916, and played rugby for Wales Secondary Schools, alongside Welsh Union legend and future Wales captain Haydn Tanner, who incidentally was Willie's cousin. He progressed to play for Swansea, and in 1935 played for the Swansea side who beat the supposedly 'unbeatable' All Blacks 11–3. Willie and Haydn were the half-backs who orchestrated this great win, and were still only teenagers. From 1937 to 1939 he won five Welsh rugby union caps and in 1939 scored the last 'four-pointer' drop goal in the five nations. Shortly afterwards he was on his way through to play rugby league, joining Bradford Northern.

During the war, he served in the Royal Air Force, which restricted his playing activities, but managed to captain a Welsh union side which beat England at the St Helens ground, Swansea which was attended by over 20,000 spectators. In 1944 he was selected to captain the Rugby League XV who beat a Rugby Union XV 15–10 at Odsal in a charity match played under union rules, but missed the match.

He won the Lance Todd Trophy when Bradford won the Challenge Cup in 1947, and was part of the great post-war Bradford Northern team. He had signed for Northern in 1939 because Harry Hornby had found him a teaching job in the city. He played 237 games for the club, scoring 55 tries and 2 goals.

He won nine Welsh rugby league caps. On the 1946 tour he only played in the New Zealand test, he went on to play twice against the Australians when they toured Britain in 1948. Like the majority of Welsh backs of that era he had a devastating dummy, which caused havoc to opposing defences, and had bullet like acceleration.

He retired from the game in 1950 to concentrate on teaching, and had a long career in education, although he was banned by the RFU from coaching youngsters at rugby union because he was a former league professional.

In 2000 the Bradford Bulls selected their 'Millennium Masters', and Willie Davies was declared to be the club's finest stand-off. His achievements in rugby union mean that he is still fondly remembered in Wales, despite his switching codes to rugby league.

### Joe Egan Hooker

*Born 19 March 1919.*
*Weight 13 stone. Height 5 feet 8 inches.*

Joe Egan started playing at that supreme nursery of Wigan rugby league players, Wigan St Patricks. After playing at full-back, a teacher suggested he play hooker and that is where he stayed. He was signed by his home town club and made his first team debut on 8 October 1938, on a winning side against Leigh. His third game was the Lancashire Cup Final against Salford. Wigan won 10–7 at Swinton. He was exempted from war service and captained Wigan during that time.

After the war he missed out on the Challenge Cup Final defeat by Wakefield as he was with the tourists on the way to Australia. He went on to make 362 appearances for the club, scored 28 tries, 12 goals for a total of 108 points. He left to join Leigh in 1950 as player-coach for a world record transfer fee of £5,000. At Hilton park, he played 104 matches, scoring 6 tries and one goal before retiring as a player in 1955.

He won a total of 14 Great Britain caps, 21 English caps and played 10 times for Lancashire. He returned to Wigan as coach in 1956 until 1961, and took the side to Wembley three times before moving to Widnes and taking them to Wembley in 1964. He had a short spell at Blackpool Borough before finally retiring from the game. At the time of writing he lives in the north-west, and spends part of the year in the Bahamas with his daughter.

### Trevor Foster Second-row

*Born: 3 December 1914. Died: 2 April 2005.*
*Weight 13 stone 10 pounds. Height 6 feet.*

Trevor Foster was born in Newport, Monmouthshire, and quickly made a name for himself playing for Newport schoolboys, Newport Hibernians and Pill Harriers before joining Newport RFC. He played in a trial for the Wales national team before he signed for Bradford Northern in 1938 for £400. He was disappointed not to have won a Welsh rugby union cap, but did play in wartime internationals for Wales.

He went on to play 438 games for Bradford, usually in the second-row, but occasionally at loose-forward. He scored an amazing 130 tries for his club. His highest in a season was 22 in 1947–48. He also scored six tries in one game. He was Bradford's outstanding forward in the post-war years, and scored in both their winning Challenge Cup finals in 1947 and 1949. He also played in five Championship Finals and six Yorkshire Cup Finals.

He retired as a player in 1955, and was then involved in coaching at Bradford and Leeds. He had been appointed as the RFL's first national coach in 1950, but resigned as he wished to continue his playing career.

Due to the war years and injuries he was limited to three Great Britain caps, although he played 16 times for Wales, seven as captain. He was awarded the prestigious Tom Mitchell Trophy in 2001 by the Rugby League Lions Association for his achievements on and off the field in enhancing the reputation of the British Lions.

Trevor, along with Joe Phillips, was the leading figure in reviving the Bradford club in 1964 after it had collapsed in 1963. He was a lifelong servant of the club up to his death in 2005.

Outside the game, Trevor worked as an Educational Welfare Officer. He played a major role in community life in Bradford, particularly with the Bradford Police Club for Young People, and the Catholic Church. He received the MBE and Papal Medal for his work in the community.

**Ken Gee** Prop Forward

*Born 1916. Deceased.*

*Weight 15 stone 3 pounds. Height 5 feet 9 inches.*

Ken Gee signed for Wigan in 1933. He played for the club in three decades – the 1930s, 1940s and 1950s. Only one other player, Jim Sullivan, has beaten Ken's record of 559 appearances for the Lancashire club. He was also a good goalkicker, kicking 508 goals and scored 54 tries. He featured in Wigan's Championship wins of 1946–47 and 1949–50 as well as their Challenge Cup victories of 1948 and 1951. He also went on to win seven Lancashire Cup winner's medals. He missed the 1946 Challenge Cup and Championship Finals as he was on the Lions tour.

Along with his club mate Joe Egan he figured in a powerful Great Britain scrum, and played in all nine matches of three consecutive Ashes series against Australia, including the 1950 Lions tour. Recently a poll of the outstanding players of the 1950s was carried out in Australia and both Gee and Egan were both selected.

He retired in August 1954, aged 37. His name is remembered through the Ken Gee Cup, played for by amateur clubs in Wigan.

**Willie Horne** Stand-off

*Born: January 1922. Died: 23 March 2001.*

*Weight 11 stone 2 pounds. Height 5 feet 7 inches.*

Willie was born in Barrow-in-Furness and without doubt is the greatest player for his home town club. After playing two trial games for Oldham, he signed for Barrow for a payment of £100 in 1943. On 13 March that year he played the first of his 461 games for the club, at St Helens. Although slight of build he was quick and elusive. His greatest skill was to split defences with perfectly timed passes so his team mates could score.

He was a good goalkicker and landed 739 goals for his club to go with the 112 tries he scored for Barrow. Besides his talent at rugby he was also an outstanding cricketer. Lancashire CCC was interested in signing him.

In 1945 he won the first of his 14 England caps. Following the 1946 tour he was again chosen for Great Britain in 1950, but sadly suffered injury, making only five appearances. In 1952 he was captain when Great Britain regained the Ashes. There was shock when he was not chosen for the 1954 tour. He played 14 times for Lancashire between 1945 and 1954.

Willie led Barrow to their only Challenge Cup victory at Wembley in 1955, beating Workington Town 21–12. He kicked five goals and a drop-goal before receiving the cup from the Duke of Edinburgh. He captained the losing Barrow sides in 1951 and 1957.

He played on until 1959 when he had become player-coach of the reserve team. In 1999 the club decided to name their new grandstand after him, which caused him to panic, thinking he was required to make a speech.

He was also made a Freeman of Barrow, and following his death in 2001, a statue of Willie was erected outside the Barrow ground. A comprehensive biography of him by Mike Gardner was published in 1994.

**Fred Hughes** Prop

*Age 30 years. Deceased.*

*Weight 14 stone 13 pounds. Height 6 feet.*

Fred 'Ginger' Hughes first played rugby union for his home town club Llanelli, before moving on to Swansea RFC. He then moved on to Cheltenham RFC where he was recruited by Barrow in late 1936. He didn't settle too quickly into rugby league and at first played mainly in the 'A' team. Prior to the war he became a regular in the first team. He earned two Welsh rugby league caps and in a surprise move in the 1945–46 season went to newly formed Workington Town. He had made 79 appearances, scoring four tries, for Barrow. He was a shock selection for the tour but wasn't selected for a test. He unfortunately suffered with gout on the Australian leg of the tour, a family inherited illness. On his return he was appointed Workington pack leader working closely with Gus Risman, but retired before their cup successes. He played 56 matches for Workington, and scored two tries.

He started a haulage contractor business carried on by his sons. His second son Emlyn became a world famous footballer, and Fred used to joke that he couldn't understand having a son as a football player. Despite that he was his son's greatest supporter.

### Dai Jenkins Scrum-half

*Age 29 years. Deceased.*
*Weight 11 stone 2 pounds. Height 5 feet 7 inches.*
Leeds had intended to sign only hooker Con Murphy from London club Streatham and Mitcham, but were persuaded by Murphy to sign his fellow Welshman Jenkins. A joint deal was done at a bargain fee of £600 in December 1936. It was expected that Jenkins would only be a reserve, but he made his debut against Bradford Northern at Headingley in January 1937 and within three months was the first choice scrum-half.

In that season he played in the Championship semi-final against Warrington. In the 1940s Dai played in all four Leeds Challenge Cup Finals, although three of them were during the war. In 1938, he had an outstanding game in the Championship Final against Hunslet, which Leeds lost.

Although Leeds only won nine league matches in the 1945–46 season, his consistent efforts earned him selection for the Lions tour. Jenkins won 17 Welsh caps, but wasn't selected for a test match on the tour. He made his test debut against New Zealand in 1947. Although he scored his side's only try in a 10–7 defeat he wasn't selected for the series decider.

Jenkins was appointed Leeds skipper in 1948–49, his final season with the club. He was awarded a joint benefit with Derek Prosser, which raised more than £800. Overall, he made 292 appearances for Leeds, scoring 55 tries and seven goals. He had spells with Keighley and Bramley before retiring in 1952.

### Albert Johnson Winger

*Born: 17 July 1918 Died: 5 August 1998*
*Weight 13 stone. Height 5 feet 10½ inches.*
Albert Johnson signed for Warrington from St Helens amateur side Pilkington Sheet Works in April 1938. He made his first team debut in a home game against Halifax on 21 January 1939 in an 11–3 win. Eight months later, the war intervened, and he only played a few games. He was on the beaches of Dunkirk when the British forces were evacuated from France in 1940.

It wasn't until peace was restored that Albert had the opportunity to really show his talent. Like the best of rugby wingmen he had the ability to sidestep an opponent without losing any speed in the process. The try he scored in the second test underlines his sheer talent where at the same time he was juggling with the ball over his head, he was able to outstrip his Australian opponent. His magnificent defence, and the way he played was truly appreciated by the Antipodeans' press.

He then went on to gain a further six Great Britain caps. He played 10 times for England, as well as representing Lancashire on four occasions. In 1949–50 he played full-back, but when Warrington reached the Challenge Cup Final at Wembley he was back on the wing as the Wire demolished local rivals Widnes 19–0 to earn their first Challenge Cup in 43 years.

Warrington's opponents not only had to cope with Johnson's speed and guile tormenting them, but on the other flank was deadly finisher Brian Bevan.

Sadly, Albert's career came to a tragic end in the 1951 Championship Final against Workington Town at Maine Road, Manchester. After only three minutes he broke his left leg, and in an era of no substitutes, he and his teammates had settle for runners-up medals in a 26–11 defeat. Even worse, the injury was so severe he never played again. Albert Johnson played 198 games for Warrington, scored 112 tries, and kicked two goals for a total of 340 points.

**Joe Jones** Full Back
*Born: Around 1919. Died January 1974, age 54.*
*Weight 12 stone 11 pounds. Height 5 feet 10 inches.*
Joe Jones was a promising player with Cilfynydd RUFC, and had played for the Glamorgan county side and Welsh Schoolboys team when he was signed by Wigan in 1936, aged 17. He signed for Barrow at the start of the 1944–45 season. While with Wigan he made 113 appearances scoring seven tries and 41 goals.

He had been seen at Wigan as an understudy for the great Jim Sullivan. He then made 221 appearances for the Barrow club, scoring four tries and 235 goals. As well as full-back, on occasions he also played at centre and stand-off. He played for Wales 12 times. His only Great Britain cap was the 1946 test against New Zealand. His last game for Barrow was in October 1952.

**Jack Kitching** Centre
*Age 24 years. Deceased.*
*Weight 13 stone 4 pounds. Height 6 feet 2 inches.*
Although born and initially educated in Bradford, Jack attended Borough Road College, London, and played rugby union. He represented Yorkshire public schools, and played for Bradford RUFC, winning a Yorkshire County cap.

He signed for Bradford Northern during the war, while still serving in the Navy. In the early part of the war his ship had been torpedoed, and he spent several hours in the water before being rescued. He made his first team debut against York on 5 February 1944, scoring two tries from the right centre position in a 44–5 victory.

He developed into one of the game's best centres, with strong driving runs, and a powerful hand-off. In the following season he played for Yorkshire and England prior to his selection for the 1946 tour.

He played in two Challenge Cup Finals, 1947 and 1949, collecting a winner's medal on both occasions. He made 171 appearances for the club, kicking two goals, and scoring 48 tries for a total of 148 points. His final appearance for Bradford Northern was in a 13–2 defeat against Halifax in 1951. He moved to Cumberland to take up a teaching post, and was involved in coaching rugby league.

**Bryn Knowelden** Centre
*Born: 27 June 1919.*
*Weight 11 stone 6 pounds. Height 5 feet 8 inches.*
Barrow born Brindle Knowelden was signed by his local club in October 1943 from a local works side. He had made his debut in September 1943.

After only 14 games of rugby league he played for England against Wales on 26 February 1944. He scored a try in a 9–9 draw, and had originally been selected as non-playing reserve for the match. In 1944–45, he again played for England against Wales, and scored a try for a Rugby League XIII against the Northern Command. He did not play for England in 1945–46, but was chosen for the tour trial, and was then selected for the 1946 tour. He made his only Great Britain appearance against New Zealand on the 1946 tour.

He played his last game for Barrow in October 1947, and was transferred to Warrington for a fee of £1,400. He had made 103 appearances for Barrow, scoring 43 tries. During his four years with the Wire he made 125 appearances, including two Championship Finals in 1948 and 1951 and a Challenge Cup Final in 1950 against Widnes when they won 19–0 with Bryn scoring a try. He had moved to stand-off where he was outstanding. He made 125 appearances scoring 37 tries before leaving in 1952 to take up a role as player-coach with Hull Kingston Rovers, and retired from the game in 1955. At the time of writing he lives happily in retirement at Lytham St Anne's.

139

**Jim Lewthwaite** Winger

*Born: 10 November 1920. Died: 23 December 2006.*

*Weight 13 stone. 5 feet 11 inches.*

Jim Lewthwaite was born at Cleator Moor in Cumberland. He achieved legendary status with Barrow, and was inducted into that club's Hall of Fame when it was launched in 2001 along with fellow 1946 tourist Willie Horne.

He was a superb natural athlete and represented Cumberland at rugby union and association football as a schoolboy, and won a medal in the All-England Schools Athletics competition at the age of 13. He was nearly lost to rugby league when aged 15 he moved to Reading to work in an aircraft factory before relocating to Barrow shipyard to take up an apprenticeship. He continued to excel at football, and had trials with Blackburn Rovers and Preston North End before switching to rugby league with Barrow in March 1943, making his first team debut at St Helens.

He scored a Barrow club record 354 tries and kicked 20 goals in exactly 500 appearances from 1943 to 1957. In his final season he scored 50 tries, a club record for a season, and retired following the club's defeat by Leeds in the Challenge Cup Final, one of three Wembley appearances he made in that decade.

Despite being the leading try scorer on the 1946 tour with 25, he was unfortunate not to be selected for the test side. Surprisingly he only won one England cap. He was Barrow head coach for a spell in the 1968–69 season, and was later a club director. On retirement he turned his sporting talents to golf, and was a well known club player.

**Harry Murphy** Second-row

*Died 7 May 1981, aged 60.*

*Weight 13 stone 12 pounds. Height 6 feet.*

Harry Murphy rose through the Wakefield junior ranks as a threequarter which helped to develop his ball-handling skills, and signed professional forms for his home town club in 1937. He made his senior debut on 6 April 1940 against Featherstone Rovers. He learnt his trade in a pack containing a great amount of experience and skill. In Trinity's outstanding 1945–46 campaign he immediately attracted the international selectors' attention, earning selection for the tour. Unfortunately, it robbed him of a place in Wakefield's side against Wigan at Wembley in the Challenge Cup Final. However, he did earn a runners-up medal in the 1945 Yorkshire Cup, and a 1945–46 Yorkshire League winners medal.

After his disappointing tour he won winners' medals in the 1946 and 1947 Yorkshire Cup Finals. In the 1940s he played for Yorkshire and represented England on four occasions. He was selected for his second Lions in 1950 and made one test appearance against Australia in Brisbane.

His Wakefield career stretched into the early 1950s covering 14 seasons. He played 290 games, scoring 50 tries and in a late career change became a goalkicker, scoring 62 goals. He had a very successful benefit match in 1950 attended by 12,252, paying £815. In January 1953 he moved to Keighley.

**Bob Nicholson** Forward

*Born: 22 February 1921. Died 6 April 1977.*

*Weight 13 stone 7 pounds. Height 5 feet 10 inches.*

Bob was from Cumbria, and as a youngster found success with the Whitehaven Central School association football team. He played rugby league with Hensingham, and was signed by Huddersfield on 21 March 1939, but due to commitments in the war did not make his first team debut until 7 October 1944. He was in the RAF during the war, and played occasionally for Hensingham, and at rugby union for his unit team.

After only 10 first team rugby league matches, he won his first international cap for England against Wales on 24 November 1945. He scored England's only try in an 11–3 defeat at Swansea. He went on to win another six England caps. Illness restricted his Great Britain appearances on the 1946 tour, and he won his first test cap against New Zealand. He played twice for Great Britain against Australia in 1948.

It was in the Huddersfield pack that he had his greatest triumphs. Along with Dave Valentine and Ike Owens, they made Huddersfield into a potent side. They were League Champions in 1948–49 beating Warrington 13–12 at Maine Road in front of a world record crowd at the time of 75,194, and won the Yorkshire League title. The following year they retained their Yorkshire title but lost in the Championship Final to Wigan 20–2. He was disappointed not to be chosen for the 1950 Lions tour to Australia and New Zealand.

Bob made 180 appearances for the club scoring 46 tries and two goals. His last appearance for Huddersfield was on 28 April 1951. He then joined Whitehaven, where he played 36 matches, scored seven tries and six goals and later became a club director.

### Ike Owens Loose-forward

*Born: 7 November 1918. Died 15 October 1998.*
*Weight 14 stone 11 pounds. Height 6 feet.*

Isaac Andrew Owens was born in Pontycymmer. He developed his rugby union with local side Blaengarw, who at that time produced a string of players who made their mark in rugby league. He went to Maesteg rugby club, becoming their first Welsh international player for 25 years, however this was in the period of the phoney war, and was classed as a Red Cross International, as was his second appearance shortly afterwards.

He became a sergeant parachute instructor in the RAF and was based at Manchester. He won the Air Force Medal during the war.

He switched to rugby league in 1943, and signed for Leeds. However, he only played 17 games for them until the end of the war. After winning the first of 12 Welsh rugby league caps, he played in two rugby union victory internationals at Leicester and Richmond. Prior to the 1946 tour he had played in only 21 of 43 Leeds fixtures due to his military service.

Following his return from the tour he was made captain of Leeds. They lost to Bradford Northern in the 1947 Challenge Cup Final. The following season he led Leeds to the Yorkshire Cup Final, losing 8–7 to Wakefield Trinity after a 7–7 draw. A record 130,000 spectators watched this cup run. He played his final match for Leeds in October 1948, having scored 40 tries and three goals, in 124 appearances.

He moved to Castleford for a record £2,750 fee; but only played seven times and scored two tries, before transferring to Huddersfield for the same amount. He was now in a superb back row, comprising Dave Valentine and Bob Nicholson. He went on to win three Yorkshire League championship winners medals, winners League Championship medal, and runners up medals against Warrington and Wigan. He retired in 1952 having played 127 games for Huddersfield, scoring 20 tries. He retired to South Wales, but came back to England two years later, joining York on a free transfer, playing 25 times, scoring one try and four goals.

He settled as a publican in York, before finally returning to South Wales. He died in 1998, aged 79.

### Doug Phillips Second-row

*Born 28 June 1919. Died 28 April 2000.*
*Weight: 14 stone 7 pounds. Height 6 feet 2 inches.*

Doug Phillips was born on the day of the Versailles peace treaty, and his middle name was 'Versailles'. He played rugby union for Neath Schoolboys and played for Swansea's first team when he was aged 19. He played twice for Glamorgan and in two Welsh trials before joining the army. He played in service internationals, often with rugby league players, and for the Rugby Union XV against the Rugby League XV at Odsal in 1944.

His display in this match bought him to Oldham's attention, but it was encouragement from one of his army colleagues who was from Oldham which saw him join the club towards the end of the war.

He made his debut in a 16–0 victory over Batley on 17 February 1945. A tall and powerful second-rower, his army duties stopped him playing regularly for the club. In 1945–46 he only played seven matches for Oldham. He made his Wales debut against

141

England on 24 November 1945. It was only his sixth senior match. He was a surprise selection for the 1946 tour, but a very successful one.

However, he only played 10 more games for Oldham, with his last appearance against Featherstone on 28 December 1946. Oldham had been unable to find accommodation for him, and were finding the cost of his commuting from South Wales onerous. He was transferred to Belle Vue, and made 235 appearances for the Manchester club, scoring 28 tries. His last game was on 13 April 1953.

He made nine appearances for Wales, the last one in 1951 against New Zealand. He played for Belle Vue in the 1947–48 Lancashire Cup Final, a 10–7 defeat against Wigan.

Doug toured again in 1950, playing 12 games, including the third test in Sydney. He scored seven tries, including a hat-trick against Wellington.

He returned to South Wales when he retired from rugby league. Despite so few games for the club was regarded as the best second-row forward Oldham ever had.

### Martin Ryan Full-back
*Born: 28 August 1923. Died: 13 January 2003*
*Weight 13 stone 11 pounds. Height 5 feet 10 inches.*
Martin Ryan was a successful schoolboy player at stand-off or centre, and only started playing full-back on the retirement of Jim Sullivan. He signed for Wigan in 1940 from local amateur side St Joseph's.

He made a successful debut playing centre in a 21–0 win at Oldham on 21 September1940. His first international cap came against Wales at Central Park in 1943. Throughout the war years he played at centre before switching to full-back in the 1945–46 season. His selection for the tour, like that of his fellow Wigan players, meant he missed both Challenge Cup and Championship Finals. In 1946–47 he was a member of the Lancashire Cup winning side, but missed out on playing in the Championship Final, when Wigan beat Dewsbury 13–4. He was part of the 1947–48 Challenge Cup Final side which beat Bradford 8–3, when his tackle on Trevor Foster saved a try and kept Wigan's lead. That season he also won a second Lancashire Cup Medal.

Further Lancashire Cup medals followed in 1948–49 and 1949–50 but amazingly he was to miss a third Championship Final, this time due to being chosen for the 1950 Lions tour. He played all three test matches against Australia, who had Clive Churchill at full-back.

A bad shoulder injury affected the final stages of his Wigan career, and both Ted Ward and Jack Cunliffe were in contention for his full-back place. However, he managed to get back in the team in his last season, 1951–52 and after missing three Championship Finals he played in the winning side against Bradford Northern in a 13–6 victory. He did play a couple of games early in the 1952–53 season at the same time being awarded a benefit, ironically with Cunliffe who had been his rival for full-back. The shoulder injury finished his career at the age of 30. He had played a major role in changing the role of full-back from a purely defensive one. His counter-attacking bought a new aspect to the position.

He was a director at the club before losing his place on the board during Maurice Lindsay's changes in the early 1980s.

### Ted Ward Centre
*Died in the 1980s.*
*Weight 13 stone 4 pounds. Height 6 feet.*
Ted Ward was signed by Wigan from Llanelli RFC, and made his debut at centre versus Castleford on 22 January 1938, when they won 12–5 at Central Park. He won a Lancashire Cup medal in 1938–39. Wigan beat Salford 10–7 in the Final. Then the Second World War interrupted his career and did not play for Wigan until the 1945–46 season. At first he had to fight for his place in the side, Wigan had a good season reaching the Championship, Lancashire and Challenge Cup Finals but Ted did not play in any of them. He wasn't selected for the Lancashire Cup Final and missed the Championship and Challenge Cup matches as he was on route for Australia.

142

Although Wigan won the Championship Final the loss of Ward was to prove disastrous in the Challenge Cup Final. Brian Nordgren, his replacement as goalkicker missed all his seven attempts at goal as Wigan lost 13–12 to a last minute Wakefield penalty.

With the return of tourists Ward, Egan, Gee and Ryan the Wigan side were continual winners. 1947–48 saw them win the Challenge Cup and Lancashire Cup and 1948–49 the Lancashire Cup. Ted Ward's goalkicking was pivotal to Wigan's success, and he was the League's leading goal kicker in both seasons, with 141 and 155 goals respectively.

In the 1949–50 season he lost his regular place in the side, playing just 12 games. There was a lot of competition for a centre berth, he took the decision to move to full-back. With Martin Ryan being called up for the 1950 Australian tour he was in the team at full-back when Wigan won the Championship Final. This was a remarkable win. Wigan had eight players in the Lions party, and still managed to beat Halifax in the semi-final after a replay, and then beat Huddersfield 20–2 in the Final before a 65,065 crowd at Maine Road.

He continued at full back and played a few times there at the start of 1950–51, but was never really able to call the position as his own, and eventually found himself as third choice. In 1951–52 he went to play for a new side in Cardiff. They only lasted the one season, and Ted decided to retire as a player, but did return to Wigan as coach from 1953 until the end of the 1955–56 season, resigning following a trophy-less spell. During his time as coach, Billy Boston joined the club, so all was not darkness and gloom. He subsequently returned to South Wales.

## Ernest Ward Centre
*Born 30 July 1920. Died: 9 July 1987*
*Weight 13 stone. Height 5 feet 11 inches.*
Bradford could have hardly known in July 1936 when they signed Ernest, a gangly youth from junior circles, what a superb investment they had made, and what a great servant to the club and his country he would become. Ernest was from Dewsbury, and came from a rugby league playing family. His father had played centre for Dewsbury, and had been a member of the team which won the Challenge Cup in 1912.

Ernest was Bradford's leader in the club's glory days of the 1940s. He led the side by example, and was also a superb player. Supporters were always amazed at his coolness and calmness when on the rare times that wonderful side were under pressure. An added bonus for Bradford was having his brother Donald playing at scrum-half, although two brothers could hardly have been different in stature and build.

He made 391 appearances for the club, and in that time scored 117 tries and 538 goals for a total of 1,427 points. In the 1949 Challenge Cup Final he was awarded the Lance Todd trophy for his man-of-the-match performance in a 12–0 defeat of Halifax which saw a then record attendance at Wembley for a Challenge Cup Final of 95,050.

He had captained Bradford to two Challenge Cup victories in 1946–47 and 1948–49, and defeat to Wigan in 1947–48. They were also twice runners-up in Championship Finals in 1947–48 and 1951–52. There were also three Yorkshire Cup triumphs, and a Yorkshire League win in 1947–48.

During the war he had played for Bradford in Championship wins in 1940–41 and 1944–45, and a Challenge Cup win in 1944. They also won the Yorkshire Cup in 1940–41, 1941–42 and 1943–44.

He made 20 test appearances for Great Britain, and was captain of the Great Britain side on the 1950 Lions tour. He kicked 22 goals in test matches. He played 20 times for England and made 11 appearances for Yorkshire.

In 1953 he left Bradford Northern to join Castleford as player-coach. He played 78 games for the Tigers, scoring nine tries and 134 goals. His playing career ended with Batley in 1956, where he played five games on loan.

**Frank Whitcombe** Prop Forward

*Born 5 June 1913. Died in 1958.*

*Weight 17 stone 8 pounds. Height 5 feet 10 inches.*

Frank Whitcombe was born in Cardiff. He was signed by Broughton Rangers in 1935. The club helped buy him out of the army, where he had played rugby union for the Army against the RAF.

He was transferred to Bradford Northern in 1938, after being spotted by Harry Hornby who was building up a team that would be dominant after the war. Like his fellow countrymen who were signed around the same time, Willie Davies and Trevor Foster, he would be a key part of the club's future success.

During the war he was a major part of Bradford's successes, with three Championships, the Challenge Cup and Yorkshire Cup wins.

With the return of peace it was clear that Frank was playing a leading part in ensuring the Bradford pack won a good supply of the ball. Despite his considerable bulk he was extremely light on his feet, and very dangerous around the scrum. He was a key part in the club's successes in the 1940s.

His selection for the 1946 tour was no surprise, and with the selectors decision to only select 11 forwards it was fortunate that Whitcombe's great power and stamina was available when injuries hit the tourists' forwards. His greatest moment was in the 1948 Challenge Cup defeat by Wigan, and despite being on the losing side he was awarded the Lance Todd Trophy for man-of-the-match. He was the first player on a defeated team to win this award, and over the years very few prop forwards have won it. He is also (up to 2008) the oldest player to have won the Trophy.

His only two test caps were won on the 1946 tour, but Frank represented Wales 14 times. He retired at the end of the 1948–49 season, having won the Challenge Cup for the second time.

For a time he was a director of Bradford Northern as well as being a popular mine host in one of Bradford's city pubs. Old Australian rival Arthur Clues who signed for Leeds was a regular customer, and became good friends. He died suddenly in 1958, in his mid 40s.

**Les White** Forward

*Born: 7 April 1923. Died 4 September 1997.*

*Weight 13 stone 7 pounds. Height 5 feet 11 inches.*

Les White started his rugby league career at York. He is one of only seven York players to play for Great Britain. In *Thrum Hallers* Robert Gate says that "Les was not the biggest forward, but he had drive, dynamism and that vital ingredient, pure class." He played in the second row, and was one of the successes of the 1946 tour, playing in all four test matches. In 1947, he moved to Wigan for a £1,900 transfer fee, the record for a forward then. He played two more tests while at Wigan, both against New Zealand in 1947. While with the Lancashire side he won a Challenge Cup and Lancashire Cup medal in 1947–48. He played for two seasons at Central Park, making 69 appearances and scoring 26 tries.

In September 1949 he moved to Halifax, for £3,000 – a club record at that time. He made his debut on 3 September against Liverpool Stanley, and made 120 appearances scoring 30 tries. He missed out on any more club honours, being part of a losing semi-final team in the 1950 Championship, and in 1953 being injured in the Championship semi-final win over Bradford Northern. He missed the Final against St Helens. His final game was at the start of the 1953–54 season, when a knee injury forced him to retire. As well as representing Great Britain, he played for England and Yorkshire.

144

# Appendix: Australian test players

### Joe Jorgenson
*Captain (first and third tests) and centre. Age 24.*
Played for Balmain, and first represented New South Wales in 1941, playing centre. His main strength was having a rock-like defence. Chosen as captain in the first test, and following the 'Kitchen' incident, although it was denied at the time, lost the captaincy in the second test. However, injury to his replacement forced the selectors to reinstate him with the captaincy for the third test. Known as a superb goalkicker, this talent deserted him in the tests. These were his only test match appearances for Australia.

He scored two tries in Balmain's 1946 Premiership win, including the decisive try. Balmain had won the Premiership Final in 1944, and had been runners-up in 1945. Jorgensen left Sydney to join Junee as player-coach, but returned to Balmain and won his place back to play in the 1947 Final, scoring all their points in a 13–9 win. He stayed at Balmain until 1953, and then finished his career with a short spell at Parramatta in 1954. He had turned down a substantial offer from Huddersfield to play in the 1946 test series. He died in 1993, aged 71.

### Ron Bailey
*Centre and captain (second test). Age 30.*
Described in the first test match programme as the 'veteran' of the side, and was a brilliant centre. Played for Newcastle against the Lions in 1936, and then played for Newtown. He joined Huddersfield in December 1937, and stayed until the end of the 1939–40 season. On returning to Australia joined Waratah-Mayfield. In 1941 he became captain-coach of Canterbury-Bankstown. He was captain of New South Wales in 1946, and took over from Jorgensen as the Australian captain in the second test. He missed the third test through injury, and the two matches against the Lions were his only test appearances. After the 1946 Premiership Final finished his career with West Maitland.

### Jim Armstrong
*Prop. Born in 1917, died in 1981.*
A big man who weighed over 16 stone, and like Frank Whitcombe was very fast. He played with South Sydney from 1939 to 1947. It was almost impossible to stop him when near the try line. He was selected for the third test, and could feel hard done not to be chosen for the second test after being reserve in the first. Prior to the second test, he had been outstanding in the inter-state game. The third test was his only international appearance.

Armstrong played as an amateur because he was also a champion wrestler, and would not have been able to compete in the Olympics if he had turned professional. He won the Bronze medal in the 1948 Olympics, Gold in the 1950 Empire Games and silver in the 1962 Olympic games, when he was well over 40 years old. He was the Australian champion seven times, and the undefeated New South Wales champion for 23 years.

### Arthur Clues
*Second-row. Born 2 May 1924. Died 3 October 1998.*
Arthur Clues was one of the great forwards of the post-war period, and another to be lost to the Australian test team through a move to British Rugby League. He joined Wests in 1943, and in 1946 was still a policeman. Without doubt, he was the star player in the Australian pack. At the end of the season, Arthur was signed by Leeds, and became an institution at Headingley. He made his debut on 1 February 1947, and immediately brightened up the air of post war austerity. The Leeds club website says he had "a combination of awesome power, lithe sidestep, tremendous acceleration, [and] majestic kicking." He was also one of the toughest players around.

He went on to make 236 appearances for the club, virtually scoring a point per game, and any promotion by the club saw Arthur involved. He played until 1954 for Leeds, before moving across the city to play for Hunslet until 1957. He played 14 times for the Other Nationalities team, and was another player in the 1946 series whose only test appearances were in that year.

On retirement, he opened a sports shop in Leeds, and always remained a larger than life personality. He lived in Leeds until he died on 3 October 1998.

### Lionel Cooper
*Left wing. Age 23.*
One of the great wingers of the post-war period, Cooper was first spotted playing Australian Rules when he was a soldier based in Darwin. Played for Eastern Suburbs, and won the award as the outstanding New South Wales player of the year in 1946. He was first approached by Leeds, but chose Huddersfield instead, winning all the major honours in the British game in a golden age for the West Yorkshire club. He still holds Huddersfield's individual try scoring record with 10 in a match – and two goals – against Keighley in 1951, and most tries in a career - 420. He led the season's try scorers in rugby league three times, finally finishing up with a career total of over 440. His record speaks for itself, but he was a wonderful player to watch, and was truly awesome close to the opposition try line. The 1946 test matches were his only appearances for Australia, but in Britain he played for the Other Nationalities team and other representative sides. He retired in 1955 and returned to Australia.

### Pat Devery
*Half-back. Age 23.*
Devery was seen has the major star of the Australian side. He played initially in Queensland, for Fortitude Valley in the Brisbane League, and was spotted by Balmain in a services match during the war. He joined them in 1944, but 1946 was his first full season of major rugby league, he had been the outstanding player in the inter-state match. Already he was seen as Australia's leading ball handler. Balmain saw Devery as the player to build around in the post-war years. This confidence was proved correct, as played in the 1946 and 1947 finals. In 1947 he was the season's top point scorer. He then joined Huddersfield for £7,000, a record contract, where he played alongside his former international colleague Lionel Cooper. He still holds the Huddersfield club record for most points in a season 1952–53 with 332. He won Championship and Challenge Cup medals with Huddersfield. He also made 11 appearances for the Other Nationalities. His three tests for Australia in 1946 were his only international appearances for the Kangaroos.

In 2005 Pat was named as one of the inductees, into the Balmain Tigers Hall of Fame. He retired from playing in 1954, and went to teach in Puerto Rico and America, where he was living in 2008.

### Trevor Eather
*Centre. Age 24.*
He was a surprise selection for the third test, his only Australian cap. He was playing for Boggabri, and had played for New South Wales in 1946. He played for Wests in 1947.

### Frank 'Bumper' Farrell
*Prop. Age 28. Died 1985.*
Popularly known as 'Bumper' Farrell, he had a fearsome reputation. In 1945 he had come close to being expelled from the game for almost biting off the ear of St George prop Bill McRitchie. Following this incident, 'Bumper' liked to assure the opposition that he had left his dentures in the dressing room. He first joined Newtown in 1936, and played for them until 1951. He made 250 appearances for the club, and became the first player to reach that number for a club in the NSWRL. He played four tests for Australia.

Despite being a policeman, he was believed to have associations with underworld figures. While this would be frowned on today, in the post-war period it added more substance to the Farrell legend. He died in 1985.

146

### Johnny Grice
*Scrum-half. Age 24.*
Grice played his club rugby league for Brisbane Souths, having joined them from Ipswich. He made four appearances for Queensland in 1945 and 1946, and was chosen for the test side after Kennedy was injured. His two appearances against the Lions were his only test caps. The match programme for the first test described him as "a resourceful player, very fast from the scrum-base and a solidly-built little fellow".

### Jack Hutchinson
*Loose-forward.*
Hutchinson played for Souths from 1943 to 1945, and for Newcastle in 1946. He played for the Country side and New South Wales in 1946, and then made his only test appearance in the second test against the Lions.

### Reg Kay
*Second-row. Age 25.*
Reg Kay was Queensland's outstanding second-rower in 1946. He played for Brisbane Southern Suburbs. A good ball handler, he came to prominence playing for the Australian Inter Forces side, and the Royal Australian Air Force side. He played in all three tests against the Lions, but they were his only appearances for Australia. In 1946 he also made his three appearances for Queensland, including the victory over the Lions.

### Clem Kennedy
*Half-back. Age 24.*
Kennedy played for South Sydney and had made his debut in 1939. His career was interrupted by the war. He played for New South Wales in 1945, and in 1946 had a season blighted by injury, which prevented him from playing at international level until the final test. A creative half-back, and although small in stature, was seen as a player to create openings for his teammates. He was selected for Australia despite his club side not winning a match all season. He subsequently joined Cessnock in 1947, before returning to the NSWRL with Newtown. His match against the Lions was his only international appearance.

### Noel Mulligan
*Loose-forward. Age 20.*
Mulligan was an emerging talent in 1946, who with his speed was seen as the player to close down Owens around the scrum base. He was unavailable due to injury for the second test, but was recalled for the third. He had joined Newtown in 1945, and played for them until 1948, with a break in 1947 when he was captain-coach of Bowral. He then joined St George for 1950 and 1951. He made 10 test appearances for Australia. After leaving St George he played in country rugby league, and in 1962 captained Southern Division to a win against the British Lions.

### Edgar Newman
*Winger. Age 32.*
Edgar Newman signed for Canterbury-Bankstown in 1938 from Cowra aged 24. He played for the club until 1944. He was back at Cowra following overseas service in the war when he played for Southern Districts against the Lions. He then played for New South Wales and made his test debut against the Lions aged 32, the oldest ever for Australia. His two appearances against the Lions were his only tests for Australia. He rejoined Canterbury-Bankstown in 1948 before having to retire through injury.

### Dave Parkinson
*Full-back. Age 23.*
The Kangaroos' full-back had a meteoric rise in major Australian rugby league. He was another Balmain player, in only his third season with the club. His great performance for

Sydney against South Coast the week before the first test made him a surprise selection for the first test. He went onto have an outstanding game, and showed great courage in the third test, playing on after an injury that was subsequently found to be a broken leg. Played in the 1944 and 1945 Balmain Premiership sides, but missed the 1946 final through injury. The 1946 series matches were his only three tests for Australia.

### George Watt
*Hooker. Age 28.*
Watt played with Eastern Suburbs, and was known as an all-action player over 80 minutes, and could be called the old man of the side. He joined Hull at the end of the 1947 season, and married a local girl, settling in the East Yorkshire city, where in 2008 he celebrated his 91st birthday.

George was one of the few pre-war players selected by the Australians, and had been a Premiership winner with Balmain in 1939 and in 1944. In 1945 he joined Easts, who beat Balmain 22–18 making George a three times Premiership winner.

With Hull he appeared 90 times, scoring nine tries and a goal, in four seasons. He briefly played for Rochdale, then came back to Australia in 1954 playing again for Balmain. He lived and worked in Sydney until 1959, then George and his family moved back to Hull. His only international appearances were in the 1946 test series.

### Roy Westaway
*Prop. Age 28.*
Westaway played for the Brisbane Valleys club. He made seven appearances for Queensland between 1940 and 1946. He played in the first two tests against the Lions, which were his only international appearances.

### Noel White
*Right wing. Age 22.*
Although having great pace, White was seen as more of a defensive type player, with a record that year in state football of never allowing his opposing winger to score. He played for Kurri Kurri in New South Wales. The third test was his only international appearance, and he never played in the New South Wales Rugby League competition.

Eric Bennett, Jack McPherson and Eric Bowe were named as reserves for the Australian team in the first and third tests, but did not play.

Of the 18 players who appeared for Australia in this series, only two, Farrell and Mulligan, won further caps. However, had Clues, Cooper, Devery and Watt not gone to play in England, it is very likely they would have won more caps.

Some research for this appendix was from the *Encyclopaedia of Rugby League Players* by Alan Whiticker and Glen Hudson.

# Appendix: New Zealand test players

### Roy Clark
*Stand-off and captain. Born 9 June 1919. Died 28 January 1999.*
Played for North Shore after switching from rugby union, and joined Auckland in 1946. Mainly played at full-back, could also play at centre and stand-off. Also played for Auckland against the Lions. Played three tests for New Zealand and was a tourist in 1947–48.

### Bob Aynsley
*Hooker. Born 5 January 1922.*
Played for West Coast from 1944 to 1951. Played for West Coast against the Lions as well as the test match. Played five tests for New Zealand, and toured Great Britain and France in 1947–48 with the Kiwis. Later became a referee.

### Warwick Clarke
*Full-back. Born 1921. Deceased.*
Played for Ellerslie and City before joining Auckland in 1943. Played 11 tests for New Zealand from 1946 to 1949, including the 1947–48 tour and four tests against Australia. Highly regarded full-back.

### Rex Cunningham
*Scrum-half. Born 11 January 1924.*
Played for City and Auckland. Played four tests for New Zealand. Toured with the Kiwis in 1947–48 and to Australia in 1948.

### Arthur Gillman
*Second-row. Born 1921. Deceased.*
Played for Addington, Canterbury, Hokitika and West Coast. Played two tests for New Zealand, and for South Island against the Lions. Had to retire prematurely from rugby league in 1948 due to a shoulder injury.

### Robert (Bruce) Graham
*Prop. Born 9 August 1920. Died 30 April 1994.*
Played his only test against the 1946 Lions, and scored the winning try. Played for North Shore and Auckland. Played rugby union while in the army during the war.

### Travers Hardwick
*Loose-forward. Born 13 March 1923. Died 25 May 1979.*
Played 14 tests for New Zealand from 1946 to 1952. Was on the 1947–48 Kiwi tour, also played twice against the 1950 Lions. Played his club rugby for Ponsonby, Auckland, Ngaruawahia and Waikato. Seen as the best loose-forward in New Zealand in the immediate post-war period. Later became a New Zealand selector, and is a New Zealand Rugby League Legend of League.

### Len Jordan
*Centre. Born 24 January 1920.*
Played eight tests as a utility back for New Zealand between 1946 and 1949. Top try scorer for the Kiwis on the 1947–48 tour. Played for Northcote, Ponsonby and Auckland from 1941. His son Chris played for the Kiwis in 1977 and 1978.

### Charlie McBride
*Second-row. Born 10 April 1925.*
Seen as one the Kiwis' best-ever second row forwards. Played 21 tests between 1946 and 1952, including two tours of Great Britain and France in 1947–48 and 1951–52.

Played for West Coast against the 1946 and 1950 Lions. Played for Blackball and Marist. He is a New Zealand Rugby League Legend of League.

### Bill Mountford
*Winger. Born 29 April 1922. Died 29 June 1991.*
Played his only test against the 1946 Lions, and for West Coast against the tourists. He played for Blackball. Usually played at centre. Later was the West Coast director of coaching and became a referee. His younger brother, Ken (Peter) Mountford also played for the Kiwis, while his older brother Ces had a distinguished career with Wigan, and subsequently coached Warrington and New Zealand.

### Jack Newton
*Prop. Born 9 March 1918.*
Could play at prop or in the second row. Played 13 tests for New Zealand from 1946 to 1950, including the 1947–48 tour. Also played against the 1950 Lions. Played for Runanga and West Coast.

### Roy Nurse
*Winger. Born 23 September 1919. Died 7 February 1991.*
Speedy winger who was born in Wales, and won his only test cap against the 1946 Lions. Apparently would have been selected for the 1939 Kiwi tourists, but his father would not buy shares in Kiwi Tours Ltd. Played for Ponsonby and Auckland.

### Maurie Robertson
*Centre. Born 19 April 1925. Died 25 May 2001.*
Played 18 tests for New Zealand from 1946 to 1952, and is regarded as one of the Kiwis' greatest centres. Toured Great Britain and France twice. Played two tests against the 1950 Lions, and was the Kiwis' captain from 1950 to 1952. Played for Richmond, Cunnamulla and Auckland. He is a New Zealand Rugby League Legend of League.

The research for this appendix was mainly done from two books: Bruce Montgomerie's *Those Who Played* and *The Kiwis – 100 years of International Rugby League* by John Coffey and Bernie Wood.

150

# Appendix: Statistics and Records

**Matches in Australia**

### Wednesday 22 May Southern Districts 4 England 36
Venue: Junee
Southern Districts: Goals: Price, Harlot.
England: Tries: Batten 2, Horne 2, Ernest Ward, Ryan, Nicholson, Risman.
Goals: Risman 6.
Attendance: 6,135.
Receipts: £649

### Wednesday 29 May Southern Tablelands (Group 8) 12 England 45
Venue: Canberra
Southern Tablelands (Group 8): Tries: Hodges, Grills. Goals: Williams 2, Tull.
England: Tries: Lewthwaite 3, Bassett 3, Kitching 3, Hughes, Murphy. Goals:
Ted Ward 6.
Attendance: 5,095
Receipts: £445

### Saturday 1 June New South Wales 10 England 14
Venue: Sydney Cricket Ground
New South Wales: Tries: Clues, Cooper. Goals: Jorgenson 2.
England: Tries: Owens, Batten. Goals: Risman 4.
Attendance: 51,634
Receipts: £6,012

### Sunday 2 June South Coast 15 England 12
Venue: Wollongong
South Coast: Tries: Ezart, Hazelton, Russell. Goals: Watts 3.
England: Batten, Whitcombe. Goals: Horne 3.
Attendance: 12,000
Receipts: £1,330

### Saturday 8 June New South Wales 7 England 21
Venue: Sydney Cricket Ground
New South Wales: Try: Cooper. Goals: Jorgenson 2.
England: Tries: Kitching, Bassett, Egan. Goals: Risman 6.
Attendance: 47,431
Receipts: £5,249

### Wednesday 12 June Western Districts 2 England 33
Venue: Orange
Western Districts: Goal: Kennerson.
England: Tries: Batten 2, Ted Ward 2, Knowelden, Owens, Lewthwaite.
Goals: Risman 6.
Attendance: 8,318
Receipts: £958

### Saturday 15 June Newcastle 18 England 13
Venue: Newcastle
Newcastle: Tries: Grave 2, Hutchinson, Whyle. Goals: Screen 3.

England: Tries: Knowelden, Ted Ward, Lewthwaite. Goals: Ted Ward 2.
Attendance: 17,134
Receipts: £2,437

### Monday 17 June Australia 8 England 8 (First Test)
Venue: Sydney Cricket Ground
Australia: Tries: Bailey, Cooper. Goal: Jorgensen.
England: Tries: Horne, Whitcombe. Goal: Risman.
Attendance: 64,527
Receipts: £10,106

### Wednesday 19 June Northern New South Wales 5 England 61
Venue: Tamworth
Northern NSW: Try: Montgomery. Goal: Hillier.*
England: Tries: Egan 3, Bassett 2, Lewthwaite 2, Knowelden 2, Owens, Jones,
Phillips, Davies. Goals: Ted Ward 11.
Attendance: 7,270
Receipts: £804
*Some reports give the goal to Elsenhuth

### Saturday 22 June Queensland 25 England 24
Venue: Brisbane
Queensland: Tries: Kenny 2, Melrose, Brosnan, Morris. Goals: Gayler 5.
England: Tries: Johnson 2, Batten 2, Egan, Kitching. Goals: Risman 3.
Attendance: 21,500
Receipts: £2,914

### Tuesday 25 June Wide Bay 12 England 16
Venue: Bundaberg
Wide Bay: Tries: Migner, Casey. Goals: Dunne 2, King.
England: Tries: Bassett, Lewthwaite, Kitching, Horne. Goals: Ernest Ward, Ted
Ward.
Attendance: 6,356
Receipts: £663

### Thursday 27 June Central Queensland 12 England 35
Venue: Rockhampton
Central Queensland: Tries: Davidson, Brighton. Goals: Brennan 3.
England: Tries: Batten 3, Knowelden, Whitcombe, White, Phillips.
Goals: Ernest Ward 6, Ted Ward.
Attendance: 7,070
Receipts: £718

### Sunday 30 June North Queensland 16 England 55
Venue: Townsville
North Queensland: Tries: Ross, Harding. Goals: Jackson 5.
England: Tries: Batten 4, Bassett 3, Horne 2, Owens 2, Risman, White, Ted
Ward, Phillips. Goals: Horne 2, Ernest Ward 2, Owens.
Attendance: 7,567
Receipts: £1,298

**Tuesday 2 July Mackay 0 England 94**
Venue: Mackay
England: Tries: Lewthwaite 7, Johnson 4, Kitching 3, Knowelden 3, Davies, Owens, Hughes. Goals: Ernest Ward 17.
Attendance: 5,044
Receipts: £568

**Saturday 6 July Australia 5 England 14 (Second Test)**
Venue: Brisbane Exhibition Ground
Australia: Try: Cooper. Goal: Jorgensen.
England: Tries: Bassett 3, Johnson. Goal: Ernest Ward.
Attendance: 40,500
Receipts: £6,009

**Tuesday 9 July Brisbane 15 England 21**
Venue: Brisbane
Brisbane: Tries: Tyquin, Schatz, Kenny. Goals: Murphy 3.
England: Tries: Davies 2, Kitching 2, Ted Ward; Goals: Ted Ward 3.
Attendance: 15,722
Receipts: £2,257

**Thursday 11 July Ipswich 12 England 29**
Venue: Ipswich
Ipswich: Tries: Brown, Stephens. Goals: Schultz 3.
England: Lewthwaite 2, Owens 2, Horne 2, Knowelden, Bassett, Egan. Goal: Horne.
Attendance: 5,237
Receipts: £803

**Saturday 13 July Toowoomba 5 England 34**
Venue: Toowoomba
Toowoomba: Tries: Bentley. Goal: Gayler.
England: Tries: White 2, Batten 2, Kitching, Hughes, Johnson, Horne. Goals: Ernest Ward 3, Risman 2.
Attendance: 9,863
Receipts: £1,281

**Tuesday 16 July North Coast 8 England 53**
Venue: Grafton
North Coast: Tries: Morcom, Gooley. Goals: Booker.
England: Tries: Kitching 3, Lewthwaite 2, Knowelden 2, Hughes, Foster, Johnson, Curran, Nicholson, Davies. Goals: Johnson 3, Owens 3, Jones.
Attendance: 6,955
Receipts: £966

**Saturday 20 July Australia 7 England 20 (Third Test)**
Venue: Sydney Cricket Ground
Australia: Try: Kennedy. Goals: Jorgensen 2.
England: Tries: Bassett 2, Curran, Owens; Goals: Risman 3, Ted Ward.
Attendance: 35,294
Receipts: £4,461

**Matches in New Zealand**

### Saturday 27 July South Island 12 England 24
Venue: Christchurch
South Island: Tries: K. Mountford, W. Mountford. Goals: Davidson, Nuttall, Ord.
England: Tries: Lewthwaite 3, Knowelden 2, Ernest Ward.
Goals: Ernest Ward 3.
Attendance: 8,000

### Monday 29 July West Coast 17 England 8
Venue: Greymouth
West Coast: Tries: Teen, Ord, K. Mountford. Goals: McNaughton 3, Nuttall.
England: Tries: Risman, Owens. Goal: Ted Ward.
Attendance: 4,000

### Wednesday 31 July Maoris 8 England 32
Venue: Wellington
Maoris: Tries: Bramley, Thompson. Goal: Hemi.
England: Tries: Ernest Ward 2, Knowelden 2, Johnson 2, Lewthwaite, Gee.
Goals: Ernest Ward 4.
Attendance: 10,000

### Saturday 3 August Auckland 7 England 9
Venue: Auckland
Auckland: Tries: Cunningham. Goals: Clarke 2.
England: Tries: Bassett 2, Nicholson.
Attendance: 20,000

### Wednesday 7 August South Auckland 12 Great Britain 42
Venue: Huntley
South Auckland: Tries: Hilton, Chell. Goals: Stevens 3.
Great Britain: Tries: Johnson 3, Nicholson 2, White 2, Jenkins, Lewthwaite, Kitching. Goals: Ted Ward 6.
Attendance: 3,000

### Saturday 10 August New Zealand 13 England 8 (Test match)
Venue: Carlaw Park, Auckland
New Zealand: Try: Graham; Goals: Warwick Clarke 5.
England: Tries: Batten, Ernest Ward. Goal: Ernest Ward
Attendance 10,000

### Monday 12 August Auckland 9 England 22
Venue: Carlaw Park, Auckland
Auckland: Tries: Nurse: Goals: Clarke 3.
England: Tries: Lewthwaite, Kitching, Johnson, Owens. Goals: Ernest Ward 5.
Attendance: 12,400

## In Australia

| P | W | D | L | F | A |
|---|---|---|---|---|---|
| 20 | 16 | 1 | 3 | 638 (146 T, 100 G) | 198 (36 T, 45 G) |

## In New Zealand

| P | W | D | L | F | A |
|---|---|---|---|---|---|
| 7 | 5 | 0 | 2 | 145 (35 T, 20 G) | 78 (12 T, 21 G) |

## Overall

| P | W | D | L | F | A |
|---|---|---|---|---|---|
| 27 | 21 | 1 | 5 | 783 (181 T, 120 G) | 276 (48 T, 66 G) |

| Players | P | T | G | Pts |
|---|---|---|---|---|
| Arthur Bassett (Halifax) | 11 | 18 | 0 | 54 |
| Eric Batten (Bradford Northern) | 13 | 18 | 0 | 54 |
| George Curran (Salford) | 16 | 2 | 0 | 6 |
| Willie Davies (Bradford Northern) | 14 | 5 | 0 | 15 |
| Joe Egan (Wigan) | 17 | 6 | 0 | 18 |
| Trevor Foster (Bradford Northern) | 10 | 1 | 0 | 3 |
| Ken Gee (Wigan) | 18 | 1 | 0 | 3 |
| Willie Horne (Barrow) | 14 | 9 | 6 | 39 |
| Fred Hughes (Workington Town) | 13 | 4 | 0 | 12 |
| Dai Jenkins (Leeds) | 11 | 1 | 0 | 3 |
| Albert Johnson (Warrington) | 17 | 15 | 3 | 51 |
| Joe Jones (Barrow) | 11 | 1 | 1 | 5 |
| Jack Kitching (Bradford Northern) | 12 | 17 | 0 | 51 |
| Bryn Knowelden (Barrow) | 13 | 15 | 0 | 45 |
| Jim Lewthwaite (Barrow) | 15 | 25 | 0 | 75 |
| Tommy McCue (Widnes) | 15 | 0 | 0 | 0 |
| Harry Murphy (Wakefield Trinity) | 1 | 1 | 0 | 3 |
| Robert Nicholson (Huddersfield) | 11 | 5 | 0 | 15 |
| Ike Owens (Leeds) | 18 | 11 | 4 | 41 |
| Doug Phillips (Oldham) | 18 | 3 | 0 | 9 |
| Gus Risman (Salford) | 14 | 3 | 31 | 71 |
| Martin Ryan (Wigan) | 4 | 1 | 0 | 3 |
| Ernest Ward (Bradford Northern) | 16 | 5 | 43 | 101 |
| Edward (Ted) Ward (Wigan) | 12 | 5 | 32 | 79 |
| Frank Whitcombe (Bradford Northern) | 19 | 3 | 0 | 9 |
| Les White (York) | 18 | 6 | 0 | 18 |

# Appendix: The tour finances

(All sums rounded to £ only)

**Gate receipts**
| | |
|---|---|
| Australia | £49,937 |
| New Zealand | £9,300 |
| **Total** | **£59,237** |

**Tax payable**
| | |
|---|---|
| Australia | £11,710 |
| New Zealand | £1,214 |
| **Total** | **£12,925** |

**Net gate receipts**
| | |
|---|---|
| Australia | £38,226 |
| New Zealand | £8.085 |
| **Total** | **£46,312** |

**England's share**
| | |
|---|---|
| Australia | £22,931 |
| New Zealand | £4,851 |
| **Total** | **£27,782** |

**Host's shares**
| | |
|---|---|
| Australia | £15,295 |
| New Zealand | £3,234 |

**Financial summary**
| | | |
|---|---|---|
| Share of gate receipts | | **£27,792** |
| Allowances to players & dependents | £3,725 | |
| All other expenses | £10,871 | |
| Exchange difference | £3,548 | |
| **Total costs** | | **£18,145** |

| | |
|---|---|
| **Profit** | **£9,647** |
| One third share to players | £3,215 |
| Two thirds to RFL | £6,431 |

Each player received a bonus from the profits of £123/13/7. Some of this money was paid to the players during the tour, the balance was paid on their return home. RFL Secretary Bill Fallowfield noted in his financial report to the RL Council that the allowances to the players and their share of the profits amounted to £6,940/16/9, which was more than the RFL had made from the tour. He also said that the gate receipts were £10,028/7/5 higher than the 1936 tour, but the expenses and allowances were higher on this tour.

Our thanks to Simon Foster for providing a copy of the financial report of the tour.

# Bibliography

## Books and pamphlets

*100 years Maori Rugby League* John Coffey and Bernie Wood (Huia Publishers, Wellington, 2008)
*A Centenary of Rugby League* Ian Heads and David Middleton (Pan Macmillan, Sydney 2008)
*Arthur Clues* Maurice Bamford (Vertical Editions, Skipton, 2008)
*"Bob"* [Nicholson] A.N. Gaulton (Huddersfield C&AC SC, Huddersfield)
*"Keeping the Dream Alive" – Barrow RFC* Dave Huitson, Keith Nutter & Steve Andrews (Self published, Barrow, 2008)
*England to Australia and New Zealand* Eddie Waring (F. Youngman Ltd, Leeds)
*Essential Australia* (AA World Travel Guides)
*History of Rugby League No.51 1945-46* Irvin Saxton (Ed) (*Rugby Leaguer /* Irvin Saxton, Pontefract)
*Huddersfield RLFC 100 Greats* David Gronow (Stadia, Stroud, 2008)
*Our Game* (Issue 6) Peter Lush & Dave Farrar (London League Publications Ltd, London, 2002)
*Rugby League test matches in Australia* Alan Whiticker and Ian Collis (ABC Books, Sydney NSW 2001)
*Rugby Renegade* Gus Risman (Stanley Paul, London, 1958)
*The Encyclopaedia of Rugby League Players* Alan Whiticker and Glen Hudson (Gary Allen, Smithfield NSW, 1999)
*The Kiwis* John Coffey and Bernie Wood (Hodder Moa, Auckland, 2007)
*The Second World War in the Far East*, H.P. Wilmott (Cassell & Co. 1999)
*The Struggle for the Ashes II* Robert Gate (Self published, Ripponden, 1996)
*Those Who Played* Bruce Montgomerie (Montgomerie Publishing, Sydney 2004)
*Trevor Foster* Simon Foster, Robert Gate and Peter Lush (London League Publications, London, 2005)

## Newspapers

*Brisbane Times*
*Daily Herald*
*Manchester Guardian*
*Rugby Leaguer*
*Search* (Sydney)
*Sunday Pictorial*
*The Courier Mail* (Brisbane)
*The Sunday Mail* (Sydney)
*The Sunday Telegraph* and *Daily Telegraph* (Sydney)
*The Sydney Morning Herald*
*The Sydney Sunday Sun and Sydney Sun*
*Truth* (Sydney)
*Yorkshire Evening Post*
*Yorkshire Post*

**A new edition of *Rugby League Review*, with articles on the game's history, current issues, international coverage, book reviews and obituaries.**

Published in September 2008 at £12.95, order for just £12.00 post free from www.llpshop.co.uk (credit card orders) or by cheque from London League Publications Ltd, PO Box 10441, London E14 8WR

# Peter Fox
## The players' coach

Peter Fox was involved in professional rugby league for almost 50 years. After playing for Sharlston Rovers, he had a 13 year playing career with Featherstone Rovers, Batley, Hull KR and Wakefield Trinity, he became one of British rugby league's most successful coaches.

Highlights of his coaching career include:

- Coaching Great Britain and England, including beating the Australians in 1978
- Winning eight matches with Yorkshire
- Winning the Challenge Cup and promotion with **Featherstone Rovers**
- Winning the First Division title in 1980 and 1981 with **Bradford Northern**
- Winning promotion with **Bramley**
- Winning the Premiership, Yorkshire Cup and John Player Trophy

With a foreword by David Hinchliffe, this authorised biography, published in June 2008 and based on extensive interviews and research, gives the inside story of Peter's at times controversial rugby league career. It includes how he developed the teams he coached, and the players he signed. Every rugby league fan will find it of great interest.

Special offer for readers of this book: £14.00 post free (cover price £14.95). Credit card orders via www.llpshop.co.uk or from PO Box 10441, London E14 8WR (Cheques payable to London League Publications Ltd). The book can also be ordered from any bookshop at £14.95. (ISBN: 9781903659397)

## All local lads
### St Helens and Pilkington Recs RLFC
### By Alex Service and Denis Whittle

The full story of the only works team ever to play in professional rugby league. From their early days in rugby union, to association football, St Helens Recs and then the post-war amateur Pilkington Recs, a fascinating tale of triumph, tragedy and survival against the odds.

Published in November 2008 at £13.95. Available direct from London League Publications Ltd for

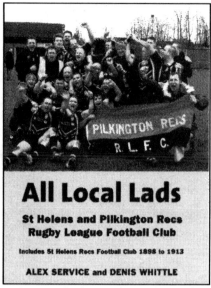

£13.00, post free. Credit card orders via www.llpshop.co.uk or by cheque payable to London League Publications Ltd to PO Box 10441, London E14 8WR. Or order from any bookshop for £13.95 (ISBN: 9781903659434)

## Liverpool City RLFC
### By Mike Brocken

Rugby league in Liverpool has a long history. Older fans have memories of visits to watch Liverpool Stanley before the war and Liverpool City in the 1950s and 1960s. This history of rugby league in Liverpool covers from the 1850s to the present day. It includes the first Liverpool City RLFC, Wigan Highfield and London Highfield, the forerunners to Liverpool Stanley RLFC, and the club after it moved to Huyton in 1969 until it was wound up in 1997.

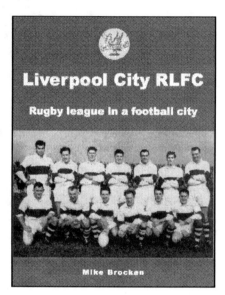

Published in October 2008 at £14.95.
Order from London League Publications for £14.00 post free. Credit card orders via www.llpshop.co.uk or by cheque payable to London League Publications Ltd to PO Box 10441, London E14 8WR. Or order from any bookshop for £14.95 (ISBN: 9781903659403)